Praise for *Dancing with Dynamite*

D0390388

"In *Dancing with Dynamite*, journalist Ben [...] reporting on progressive changes that have s[...] [...] past decade, exploding many myths about Latin America that are all-too-often amplified by the corporate media in the United States. Read this much-needed book." —**Amy Goodman**, *Democracy Now!*

"*Dancing with Dynamite* gives a strong sense of the vibrant social activism underway in many different countries of Latin America, as well as the complex relationship between social movements and the radical leaders that they have helped put into power. A recommended read for anyone interested in the possibilities of social change in Latin America today." —**Sujatha Fernandes**, Graduate Center of the City University of New York

"For more than a decade, social activists in North America and Europe have gained confidence that a new world is possible in light of the dynamic social movements in Latin America, particularly those of the Indigenous Peoples, but have not figured out how to apply the strategies of those movements to situations in the North. *Dancing with Dynamite* provides profound insights and a guide to how that might be done. Ben Dangl has earned a reputation as a tireless and reliable connection between two worlds, and this book is essential reading at the right moment." —**Roxanne Dunbar-Ortiz**, author of *Roots of Resistance*

"Perhaps the most important book this year, *Dancing with Dynamite* is a roadmap for social change from the bottom up. Backed by years of travel, extensive research, and powerful story-telling, Ben Dangl's book carries us across the Americas, deep into the movements making waves in South America's most radical countries. We are reminded that we in the United States have much to learn from our southern sisters and brothers." —**Michael Fox**, co-director of *Beyond Elections: Redefining Democracy in the Americas*

"Ben Dangl's *Dancing with Dynamite* incisively focuses on the relationship between social movements and governments in South America, providing a vital contribution toward understanding the region's current politics. While South American presidents receive much of the credit for the progressive changes taking place in the region, many of these changes occur largely through the heroic and courageous efforts of grassroots activists.... Dangl provides a valuable history and analysis of the largely ignored struggles of South American social movements in their fight for a better world." —**Greg Grandin**, author of *Empire's Workshop*.

"The story of the dramatic turn to the left in Latin America over in the past decade is now well known, but an equally significant story of divisions between social movements and electoral politics remains largely untold. Combining a broad knowledge of Latin America with direct experiences on the ground, journalist Ben Dangl examines the tensions that grassroots activists have felt with the progressive governments they helped put into place. With compelling prose, *Dancing with Dynamite* takes us across South America, and then draws parallels between those movements and similar struggles in the United States. Along the way, Dangl provides an expert introduction to social movements in Latin America, as well as a probing political analysis of electoral paths to social justice." —**Marc Becker**, Truman State University

"Dangl brings complicated politics to life by infusing them with the magic, mystery and unbridled joy that invigorate social movements and permeate Latin American life in general. You hear the pounding drums and smell the sizzling llama meat at Carnival in Bolivia; you feel the steam rising off baking bricks at the worker-run ceramics plant in Argentina; you taste the yerba mate and quiver with the sense of possibility in a cluttered Frente Amplio meeting room in Uruguay. It all adds up to the wondrously explosive 'dynamite' of human passion and determination that has toppled repressive right-wing regimes and now swirls in the complicated dance Dangl so deftly describes." —**Kari Lyderson**, author of *Revolt on Goose Island*

"At the end of the first decade of the 21st century, the panorama of Latin American social movements is very different from what we knew ten or twenty years ago. Now they navigate in much more tranquil waters than those agitated by the neoliberal wave. However, these seas are cloudier, less transparent, making understanding reality a much more complex task.... *Dancing with Dynamite* dares to navigate these cloudy waters, something which increasingly fewer thinkers and activists dare to do, but which turns out to be urgent." —**Raúl Zibechi**, author of *Dispersing Power*

Dancing with Dynamite

Social Movements and States in Latin America

Dancing with Dynamite

Social Movements and States in Latin America

by Benjamin Dangl

AK PRESS

EDINBURGH • OAKLAND • BALTIMORE

Dancing with Dynamite: States and Social Movements in Latin America
© 2010 Benjamin Dangl
This edition © 2010 AK Press (Oakland, Edinburgh, Baltimore)

ISBN-13: 978-1-84935-015-0 | Ebook ISBN: 978-1-84935-046-4
Library of Congress Control Number: 2010925752

AK PRESS   AK PRESS
674-A 23rd Street   PO Box 12766
Oakland, CA 94612   Edinburgh, EH8 9YE
USA   Scotland
www.akpress.org   www.akuk.com
akpress@akpress.org   ak@akedin.demon.co.uk

The above addresses would be delighted to provide you with the latest AK Press distribution catalog, which features the several thousand books, pamphlets, zines, audio and
video products, and stylish apparel published and/or distributed by AK Press. Alter-
natively, visit our web site for the complete catalog, latest news, and secure ordering.

Visit us at www.akpress.org *and* www.revolutionbythebook.akpress.org.

Printed in Canada on acid-free, recycled paper with union labor.
Cover by John Yates (stealworks.com)

Contents

Introduction

The motorcycle thundered off the highway onto a jungle road of loose red dirt framed by trees, families lounging in front of their farmhouses, and small herds of disinterested cows. We pulled up to a dusty store to buy food for our stay in the rural community of Oñondivepá, Paraguay, and asked the woman behind the counter what was available. She nodded her head, picked up a saw, and began hacking away at a large slab of beef. We strapped the meat and a box of beer on to the back of the motorcycle and roared off down the road.

A volleyball game was going on when we arrived in the area where landless activist Pedro Caballero lived. His wife offered us fresh oranges while his children ran around in the dirt, playing with some wide-eyed kittens. The sun had set, so Caballero's wife lifted a light bulb attached to a metal wire onto an exposed electric line above the house, casting light on our small gathering of neighbors. Suddenly, the dogs jumped to action, joining in a barking chorus, and lunged toward the edge of the woods. They had found a poisonous snake, a common cause of death in this small community far from hospitals.

"We are the landless," Caballero, a slight young man with shoulder length black hair, explained while peeling an orange for his young daughter. As a settler on the land, he works with his neighbors and nearby relatives to produce enough food for his family to survive. But he is up against a repressive state that either actively works against landless farmers, or ignores them. "No one listens to us, so we have to take matters into our own hands," he said. Caballero spoke of the need to occupy land as a last resort for survival. "The legal route isn't working, so we have to go for the illegal route, which does work."[1]

Caballero was a long-time friend and supporter of current Paraguayan President Fernando Lugo. He worked on the president's campaign, and held out hope that after taking office, Lugo would implement much-needed land reform for the thousands of landless farmers in the country. Now he believes the president has "turned his back on the sector that gave him everything." But Caballero, along with many other landless farmer leaders, has not stopped his militant actions. "Agrarian reform doesn't happen in the government ministries. It happens in the streets, in the plazas; it happens with land occupations."

He tells stories of the community's many confrontations with Brazilian landowners who are taking over Paraguayan land to grow soy—a rapidly expanding crop which, through a dangerous cocktail of pesticides, corrupt judges, and armed thugs, is displacing Paraguayan *campesinos* [small farmers] at an unprecedented rate. The threat of this toxic crop, protected and encouraged by the state, literally looms on the horizon for Caballero and his family: beyond his own small farm, a soy plantation is climbing down a neighboring hill toward the river. The pesticides used on the soy are already polluting their local water supply. So far, the community has resisted the encroachment with machetes and community organizing.

Ramón Denis, Caballero's uncle, is adamant that his self-built community will resist eviction. "We will not permit even one meter of soy in our community," Denis said. "In this community we work together. When the community is apathetic, nothing is possible. When the community moves, anything is possible."[2]

The story of Oñondivepá is part of the complicated relationship at the heart of this book: the dance between social movements and states. In this dance, the urgency of survival trumps the law, people acting based on the rights they were born with makes the state irrelevant, and anything is possible when the community moves.

Desperation tends to push people together, and a transformative and irrepressible power can grow from that bond. The situation a majority of people across South America find themselves in today is as dire as it was for many in the US during the Great Depression. John Steinbeck writes movingly of the solidarity that rose from that anguished period in *The Grapes of Wrath*:

> The causes lie deep and simply—the causes are a hunger in a stomach, multiplied a million times; a hunger in a single soul, hunger for joy and some security, multiplied a million times; muscles and mind aching to grow, to work, to create, multiplied a million times... The danger is here, for two men are not as lonely and perplexed as one. And from this first "we" there grows a still more

dangerous thing: "I have a little food" plus "I have none." If from this problem the sum is "we have little food," the thing is on its way, the movement has direction. Only a little multiplication now, and this land, this tractor are ours.[3]

These words speak of the hunger that pushed people to organize, that pushed them to join unions and fight against exploitative economic systems and ideologies. Decades later, a Brazilian slum dweller, Carolina María de Jesús, writes of the poverty in her community: "Hunger is the dynamite of the human body."[4] Hunger's dynamite can be self-destructive, but it can also force people to take radical, liberating action.

Hunger pushed Bolivian miners in the Revolution of 1952 to use their dynamite as a tool to overthrow a military dictatorship. Descending into the city of La Paz on April 10, 1952, with a full moon lighting their way, miners laid siege to the city, ushering in a new government. The "reluctant revolutionaries" brought into office had to be pushed from below to enact changes in the country.[5] Miners fought and won ownership over their mines. Landless farmers occupied large estates, forcing the government to follow through with land reform. Responding to grassroots pressure, the reluctant revolutionaries granted universal voting rights and broader access to education.

At the time, the US State Department said of the revolution in Bolivia that "the whole complex of lawlessness, combined with the government's apparent unwillingness or inability to control, added to a considerable degree of anarchy in the country." Historian Vijay Prashad writes that "'anarchy' for the United States was popular democracy for the Bolivians."[6]

Still, the greedy moderates administering the Bolivian revolution from above would only go so far. Eventually, overcome by their own lust for power and pressure from Washington, they cracked down on the rebellious population. In the 1950s and the following decades, the government led a wave of violence against the same grassroots sectors that had swept it into power.

But the dynamite of public demands continued exploding. In 1964, the government sent in troops against miners in Oruro who were protesting the government's bloody crackdown on labor rights activists. A miner named Domingo spoke of the violence that began when the soldiers attacked his community: "They even entered into houses of families and took people out, forcing people into the streets in their underwear and killing them. We miners in Itos tried to defend the mines. We put up a fierce resistance with dynamite... They didn't let us leave. We made a cordon and stayed awake all night from eight until dawn." The soldiers won the battle, and Domingo has suffered from insomnia ever since.[7]

The dance between the government and the people can be explosive and tragic. It can also reap benefits for marginalized sectors of society. In 2007, decades after miners fought their traitorous government, they took to the streets again with their dynamite in Oruro. This time they had a different objective: to defend the government of Evo Morales from the violent and racist right wing, and help push through a new constitution. In this case, the interests of the movements intersected with those of the government. Their dance is emblematic of a larger relationship between movements and states across South America today.

This book deals with the dances between today's nominally left-leaning South American governments and the dynamic movements that helped pave their way to power in Bolivia, Ecuador, Argentina, Uruguay, Venezuela, Brazil, and Paraguay. The discussion surrounding the question of changing the world through taking state power or remaining autonomous has been going on for centuries. The vitality of South America's new social movements, and the recent shift to the left in the halls of government power, make the region a timely subject of study within this ongoing debate. Though often overlooked in contemporary reporting and analysis on the region, this dance is a central force crafting many countries' collective destiny.

Within the context of this book, the state is defined as an institution made up of elected and appointed officials operating in a representative government that is subjected to the limitations imposed by elections and capitalism. The social movements examined here are collections of citizens engaged in grassroots activism aimed at transforming society for the betterment of the majority of its population. Participants in social movements are united by a common purpose, agenda, campaign, or goal.

In each South American country studied here, the logic of social movements competes with that of the state. The state and governing party is, by its nature, a hegemonic force that generally aims to subsume, weaken, or eliminate other movements and political forces that contest its power. In an effort to conserve and centralize power, often the electoral needs of the party or state come before the needs of the people. As anarchist legend Emma Goldman writes, government requires "that its influence and prestige constantly grow, at home and abroad, and it exploits every opportunity to increase it."[8]

Implicit in this dance is the challenge and inherent contradiction of seeking to take over state power in an effort to change the world. As US intellectual and analyst Noam Chomsky writes, "History has proven that when popular classes takeover the state and exert their power through it, [the process] produces a new kind of tyranny."[9] This tyranny manifests itself in diverse ways. The political party, for one, redirects dissent toward consolidating state power and winning elections—in the words of sociologist John Holloway, "channeling revolt."[10] Why wait to take over the state in order to transform the world, Holloway asks. Why not change the world now?

Many South American movements make revolution a part of everyday life, not something to be postponed for an electoral victory or the seizure of state power. While they may not define themselves as such, a number of these movements are anarchist in action and belief. Anarchists, in the words of writer Rebecca Solnit, believe they "do not need authorities and the threat of violence to govern them but are instead capable of governing themselves by cooperation, negotiation, and mutual aid."[11] Such a view clashes with the concept of the state, whose legitimacy is based on an assumption that people need to be governed and subjected to a higher law for the sake of order and progress.

For movements in South America that engage the state, the relationship involves a tightrope walk between cooptation and genuine collaboration. Many times, however, cooperation with the state leads to the demobilization of social movements. For this reason, sociologist Atilio Borón, a member of the International Council of the World Social Forum, writes that movements "should not convert themselves into the transmission lines of those in power" in

exchange for positions in the government, funding, or social programs. Otherwise they may lose support among their base. He says
that movements should "refuse to be used as arms of the government."[12] During elections in particular, parties work against the
autonomy of the movements.

When facing such challenges, according to Uruguayan analyst Raúl Zibechi, it is important for movements to remain true to
their own agenda, and not water down their demands to align with
the state. Movements must expand their power, potential, spaces,
and capacities.[13] However, expanding power doesn't need to mean
becoming a part of the state's political or electoral process; rather,
it can mean working to become a sustainable movement that can
weather changing political climates. When a movement understands
the stakes and playing field in its relationship with a government
or party, knows when to apply pressure, back down and regroup, it
remains sustainable. In other cases, some movements entirely pull
away from any relations with the government to focus on their own
grassroots work.

While autonomist movements and actions are a focus of this
book, the importance of state-created initiatives, social programs,
and development projects aimed at empowering people and curtail-
ing poverty should not be underestimated. In the process of working
for a better world without a state, supporting state-based programs,
if they indeed help people achieve their long and short term goals,
can be a viable strategy. Such a position, says Chomsky, involves supporting the "enforcement of health and safety regulation, provision
of national health insurance, support systems for people who need
them, etc. That is not a sufficient condition for organizing for a different and better future, but it is a necessary condition."[14]

This book is based on the belief that public-run services are by
definition more accountable than commercial, for-profit businesses
or corporate run services, and in many cases, vital for survival. The
process of negotiating with current left-leaning governments has
posed challenges to social movements; but the region's history demonstrates that multinational corporations and right-wing governments pushing through neoliberal policies have typically been even
more devastating.

Throughout much of the 1970s and early 1980s, South America saw a wave of military dictatorships come to power that crushed labor unions, political dissidents, students, and regular citizens. Tens of thousands of people were tortured, murdered, or disappeared by regimes in a coordinated effort between dictatorships spanning the continent. This Washington-supported nightmare officially ended for many countries in the 1980s. Though the dictatorships were gone, their economic policies remained.

While dissidents at the time condemned the overt violence of the regimes, many protested the equally torturous effects of pro-corporate economic policies. In a letter investigative journalist Rodolfo Walsh sent to the Argentine junta immediately before his murder in 1977, he condemned the dictatorship's violence against Argentines. After describing the crimes of dictatorship—including murder, torture, and disappearances—he said the "greater atrocity" was the regime's economic policy, which "punishes millions of human beings through planned misery."[15] He was referring to neoliberalism.

Proponents of neoliberalism contend that government participation in the economy (state-owned businesses) or regulation of the economy (taxes that favor internally produced goods) prevents full economic growth. Neoliberal economic recommendations involve slashing government spending on public works and services, such as education, healthcare, and transportation, and advocating for the privatization of public-owned services and businesses. Neoliberal economists touted competitive capitalism as the only way to ensure the development of a free society. By limiting the authority of the government, and putting economic power into the hands of the market, neoliberal policy-makers hoped to guarantee more individual freedoms.[16]

This ideology spread with the help of willing elites and leaders in South American governments, as well as pressure from international lenders such as the World Bank and International Monetary Fund, which played a vital role in using debt to force crippling neoliberal austerity measures on governments. Therefore, many of the South American presidents' actions, today and in the past, against social movements were due in part to the constraints they found themselves in as leaders of states enmeshed in global capitalism and beholden to Washington, the financial market, military powers, corporate interests, corrupt officials, bureaucracy, and the stranglehold of debt, among other factors. Destructive measures taken by states against movements were often in response to these constrictive influences at the state level, influences which have historically made dealing with the state so problematic for movements.

While neoliberalism appealed to some South American policymakers, the results for most people were disastrous. Throughout the 1960s and beyond, nascent neoliberal economists used South America as their laboratory. In recent years, South Americans have lived the results. Instead of the promised jobs, economic mobility, and expanded freedoms, neoliberalism has increasingly concentrated wealth in the hands of a few and impoverished millions. The region's shift to the left in the recent decade is largely a response to this devastating economic ideology: voters sought an alternative, and presidential candidates promised to provide such alternatives.

The relationship among private corporations, exclusively neoliberal governments, and social movements has been widely examined, as have the ways in which the state supports and enables the often devastating activities of private corporations. This was largely the focus of my first book, *The Price of Fire: Resource Wars and Social Movements in Bolivia* (AK Press, 2007). Yet the dance between left-leaning governments and social movements is another and underinvestigated matter entirely.

The relationships between movements and states examined here takes place in a variety of contexts, and involves diverse elements, tactics, and scenarios. Some movements seek to back political candidates, to mobilize their forces to form an electoral machine designed to influence a campaign and mobilize votes. They take actions to pressure the government for concessions, policies, funding, or a change in legislature. Others strike or block roads to pressure the state into exerting its power over a private corporation. Some movements act simply to defend themselves against the repression of the state. Movements have also proven to be pivotal in the fight against the right wing, in the writing of constitutions, electoral battles, and street mobilizations. Various movements have applied all of these tactics at different points in time.

In some cases, governments in these countries brought to power by movements and social demands have completely turned their backs on movements, ignoring their proposals and demands. Others unleashed outright wars on movements, leading to harsh crackdowns on rights to assemble and protest. Some governments have worked closely with movements to develop and implement political and economic policies together, while others have sought to demobilize or coopt movements by subsuming them into the government bureaucracy through coveted jobs and threats of exclusion.

Each chapter in this book focuses on this contemporary relationship in a specific country. In Chapter 1, I discuss Bolivia's Movement Toward Socialism, a "party of social movements," and the complex relationships between various movements and the Evo Morales administration. In Chapter 2, I examine the rise and influence of Ecuador's indigenous movement and the Rafael Correa administration's betrayal of this dynamic group. In Chapter 3, I look at the Argentine *piquetero*, occupied factory, and human rights movements, their participation in the 2001–2002 uprising, and their subsequent relations with the Néstor Kirchner administration. In Chapter 4, I discuss the history of the Frente Amplio (FA) in Uruguay, both as a movement and party, and examine the interplay of grassroots and party logic within the FA's electoral successes and the administrations of Tabaré Vázquez and José Mujica. In Chapter 5, I examine the popular Venezuelan forces leading to Hugo Chávez's rise to power and the current landscape of movements, state-initiated programs, and party politics making up the Bolivarian Revolution. In Chapter 6, I look at the parallel stories of the landless movement and the Workers' Party in Brazil, and rocky relations between the two since President Luiz Inácio Lula da Silva's 2002 election. Finally, looking at Paraguay in Chapter 7, I present the campesino movement's fight against the soy business and agro-industry, and how the Fernando Lugo administration has largely worked against this movement.

The book concludes with a suggestion that lessons from South American social movements could be applied in the US by activists facing similar state, party, and economic challenges. To illustrate this proposal, I give the examples of specific actions and groups that have drawn from South American strategies, including the 2008 occupation of the Republic Windows and Doors factory in Chicago which drew from tactics in Argentina, the movements for access to water in Detroit and Atlanta, which reflected tactics and struggles in Bolivia, and the Take Back the Land movement in Florida, which organized homeless people to occupy a vacant lot and pairs homeless families with foreclosed homes, mirroring the tactics and philosophy of the landless movement in Brazil.

While South American relations with the US are not addressed here at length, a few notable events and trends deserve attention. The region's shift to the left can be attributed, in part, to a response to US imperialism. The administration of George W. Bush—according to polls, the most unpopular US president ever among Latin Americans—made alternatives to business as usual more popular than ever.[17] While Washington during the Bush Administration indeed played unpopular roles in the region, including involvement in coups in Venezuela in 2002, Haiti in 2003, and the expansion of harmful military relations throughout Latin America as part of the "War on Terror," the policies of the Barack Obama administration have proven to be not much different.[18]

Among other significant moves, the Obama administration supported the June 28, 2009 coup against democratically elected President Manuel Zelaya in Honduras, signed a deal to establish seven new military bases in Colombia, and pushed for free trade deals across the region, undermining national protections for farmers and workers. In reaction to the administrations of both Bush and Obama, regional leaders have come together to form various trade and political blocs to strengthen regional integration, their autonomy from the US, and break from a past in which the region was treated simply as Washington's backyard.[19]

While many South American governments seek autonomy from Washington, social movements in various countries seek a different kind of autonomy from the states themselves. From Paraguay to Detroit, people are working from below to build their utopia today. They know a better world can be created by walking toward it. "She's on the horizon," Uruguayan author Eduardo Galeano writes of utopia. "I go two steps, she moves two steps away. I walk ten steps and the horizon runs ten steps ahead. No matter how much I walk,

I'll never reach her. What good is utopia? That's what: it's good for walking."[20]

I hope this book contributes to our collective journey toward utopia.

Thousands of Evo Morales's supporters gathered in La Paz's Plaza Murillo on December 15, 2007 to show their support for the new constitution. Photo by: Bear Guerra

CHAPTER ONE

Bolivia's Dance with Evo Morales

The streets of Oruro were clogged with people whose bodies surged with alcohol and the unceasing beats of marching brass bands. Sweat poured from the faces of the Carnival dancers, some of whom had been stomping through the city streets for hours. Revelers sprayed aerosol cans of foam at each other, tossed water balloons, bit into dried llama meat, and snapped photos. The whole city moved with an exhausted but determinedly boisterous energy from which was hard to escape. Costumed dancers spun past depicting a synthesis of heaven and hell, where the world was tossed upside down and miners became devils.

In a fitting addition to this drama, President Evo Morales, a former llama herder and coca farmer, danced with an array of brightly dressed women whose glittering outfits blazed in flashes of press cameras. Carnival is regularly described as a drama where good triumphs over evil. But anthropologist June Nash writes that it is more of a reenactment in which "good and evil become blended."[1]

While Morales danced in the Oruro streets, another dance was going on in the politicized nation: a dance between the national government controlled by the Movement Toward Socialism (MAS), Morales's political party, and the country's dynamic social movements. In 2005, Morales was elected the first indigenous president of Bolivia—a country with an indigenous population of approximately 70 percent. Morales's history as a union organizer and activist-politician throughout the 1990s and early 2000s established him as a prominent leftist figure. He rode a wave of discontent and desire for drastic change into the presidential palace.

While political marches are a daily occurrence in the cities, it is in the countryside that the MAS receives much of its electoral and social support. To find out more about this relationship, I took a train to the rural town of Uyuni, a night's ride away from the hung-over city of Oruro. After Carnival, when the fiesta's garbage had long been pressed into the streets by the celebrating thousands, the train to Uyuni lurched reluctantly out of the station. Its musty cocoon rattled against cold tracks, past small towns where occasional streetlights brought into view an alleyway soccer game and scattered couples spilling out of bars. Out the window, the moon shone on plants that clung to dry farmland rising up toward distant mountains, framed by stars and darkness. Arriving in Uyuni near dawn, I found the town was still alive with bass-filled music rolling through the dusty air, crawling with revelers from a late night party.

The next day, I walked across the dirt roads of the town, past gaping pot holes and meandering dogs, shielding my eyes from the brightness of the sun, which was magnified by the altitude. I headed toward a radio antenna at the edge of town and pushed open the creaking metal gate in front of it. The walls of the Southern High Plains Regional Federation of Workers and Peasants (FRUCTAS) radio station were lined with posters about local campaigns against the environmental impact of mining and related water pollution. Calendars distributed from past election campaigns were tacked up alongside pictures of President Morales. Behind a desk in the front office of the radio station, Claudia Yucra talked with local teenagers about how to plan their own radio program. While they chatted, other people came in to greet their families and friends on air, and to announce political meetings, fundraisers, and the town's school and sports events.

The radio station is a center for grassroots activity not only because it shares local news, information, and analysis over the airwaves to people across the city and countryside in Quechua and Spanish, but because it brings locals together to organize their own radio programs on political, social, and cultural issues. Those who work at the radio as producers and journalists are well aware of local sentiment through years of interviews, programs, and calls in to the show from listeners.

Yucra, a young, dark haired woman who displayed a mixture of kindness and confidence, had been working at the radio since high school, spending day after day interviewing locals, training youth, and organizing programs, largely around issues related to mining and the environment in the impoverished region, notable for its geographical and political distance from the central government. I wondered, out here in quiet Uyuni, what the general perspective was on the MAS political party, at this point into its fourth year in office.

Yucra said that in the past, with previous governments and political parties, the social organizations of her region were always isolated and ignored, even when they had marches and went on hunger strikes. Now, with the MAS in power, she said, "we're seeing a very different process." Yucra explained something that was reflective of other perspectives I had heard on the grassroots level across the country: that the MAS political party arose from the social movements, and was now responsive to that fundamental base. She saw the MAS as a "political instrument" that listened to the people's proposals and advocated for them on behalf of "the peasant and working class of the country. So now there are closer relationships, relationships for collective work. The present government receives the peasant organizations' proposals and now is working toward this structure so that the bases, the people of the countryside, are also paid attention to."[2]

This analysis, coming from a political participant who had been in touch with "the peasant and working class of the country" for years, underscores the image of the MAS as a benevolent tool occupying the state structure to work for the impoverished majority. This is a view held by dozens of major social movements across the country, and has been manifested by people on the electoral level when voters head to the polls under the MAS, whether for a referendum on a MAS initiative, constitutional change, or the re-election of Morales for a second term in 2009.

But what does it mean in Bolivia, a country where the social movements have been the foremost political protagonists for nearly a decade, that it is enough to simply have an ally and advocate occupying the government? What does it mean that many movements now back a government that is beholden to global capitalism and multinational lenders, a state structure that many indigenous people claim to be colonialist, and a political party that has been mired in corruption scandals and accused of coopting social movements for electoral ends? As we will see, the complex political landscape of Bolivia offers many insights into the dance between social movements and the state.

The MAS is not just any political party, it's one that arose from social movements and has pledged, after taking power, to transform and "decolonize" the state. These goals, their inherent contradictions, alongside the power of the country's social movements, make Bolivia a fascinating and illustrative case study. Nowhere else in Latin America has a grassroots political party maintained such close ties to social movements after taking office. And nowhere else have the boundaries between the party and the social movements been so confused, with each at times working for, with, and against each other.

The nature of the dance between the movements and the state since Morales took power has been in constant flux, with some of these elements of cooptation and demobilization changing on a monthly basis. However, it is possible to describe certain trends, directions, and general characteristics. To analyze this dance it is important to understand the history of the movements leading up to Morales's election, and how the MAS grew from the grassroots into a party managing Bolivia's broken state bureaucracy.

From the Streets to the Palace

Before Morales was elected president, the social movements in the country played a very active role in shaping the country's politics. As Morales himself said in late 2008, "It is the experience and the effort of the social movements that is causing democracy to address the issues that really concern poor and needy people... Democracy is much more than a routine election every four years."[3] Indeed, democracy for many Bolivians in the years leading up to Morales's election in 2005 was full of insurrections, and nearly constant protests, strikes, and road blockades.[4]

In the mid-1980s, a neoliberal plan proposed by US economist Jeffrey Sachs led to the privatization and closure of many Bolivian mines—work spaces which formed the backbone of the country's radical workers' unions. Faced with unemployment, thousands of mining families migrated to the Chapare to grow coca to survive, while others moved to El Alto, a working class city outside of La Paz. The embers of the mining movement spread, sparking radical fires across the country. While movements in the Chapare and El Alto went on to transform the political landscape of the country, political actors and organizations in Santa Cruz emerged as a right-wing force, pushing for neoliberal policies and repression against working class movements.

The coca growers' movement led directly to the creation of the MAS. The coca leaf in Bolivia has been used for centuries in the Andes as a medicine to alleviate the pain of farming and mining work, and plays an important role in indigenous customs. The leaf is chewed and consumed in tea across the country within this wide, legal market. Over time, coca leaves and the unions that defended their production became symbols of anti-imperialism in a defense of indigenous and Bolivian culture. The US-led war on drugs targeted the production of the leaf ostensibly to curtail drug production, but also to break one of the most formidable social movements—and eventually political parties—in the country.[5]

The Bolivian coca growers' movement fought against US militarization of land and communities in the war on drugs for decades, building up a fierce union that eventually grew into the MAS party. Working through this political instrument to transform the country from positions in the government, coca growers fought to legalize coca production, organize within their communities, and eventually played a key role in the Cochabamba Water War.

In 2000, the people of Cochabamba rose up against the multinational Bechtel corporation's privatization of their water. After weeks of protests, the company was kicked out of the city and the water went back into public hands. In February 2003, police, students, public workers, and regular citizens across the country rose up against an IMF-backed plan to cut wages and increase income taxes on a poverty-stricken population. The revolt forced the government and International Monetary Fund to surrender to movement demands and rescind the public wage and tax policies, ushering in a new period of unity and solidarity between movements as civil dissatisfaction gathered heat, reaching a boiling point during what came to be called the Gas War.

The Gas War, which took place in September and October of 2003, was a national uprising that emerged among diverse sectors of society against a plan to export Bolivian natural gas via Chile to the US for $.18 per thousand cubic feet, only to be sold in the US for approximately $4.00 per thousand cubic feet. In a move that was all too familiar to citizens in a country famous for its cheap raw materials, the right-wing government in power worked with private companies to design a plan in which Chilean and US businesses would benefit more from Bolivia's natural wealth than Bolivian citizens themselves.

Bolivians from across class lines united in massive protests, strikes, and road blockades against the exportation plan. They demanded that the gas be nationalized and industrialized in Bolivia, so that the profits from the industry could go to government development projects and social programs. Neighborhood councils (FEJUVEs) in the city of El Alto, many of them with formerly unionized miners as members, banded together, blocking roads in their city located strategically above La Paz. The government fought back, shooting civilians from helicopters with semi-automatic weapons, pushing movements in the city into a fury that emboldened their resistance. By mid-October, the people were successful in ousting the repressive neoliberal President Gonzalo Sánchez de Lozada, and rejecting the exportation plan, pointing the way toward nationalization.

It was shortly after this series of conflicts that Evo Morales emerged as a serious contender in the 2005 presidential elections. Riding this wave of national discontent with an adept campaign, Morales was elected president of the country on a platform that reflected the demands of the social movements. His electoral promises focused on land reform, gas nationalization, and the convocation of an assembly to rewrite the country's constitution. In varying degrees, he followed through on all of these central campaign promises.

Since Morales's inauguration in 2006, numerous movements have mobilized in defense of MAS legislation and to pressure right-wing politicians for reform. The MAS has used this movement support as a political tool, requesting grassroots action and pressure as a tactic and excuse to push legislation through under complicated circumstances—such as a boycott by right-wing politicians. One illustrative example of this collaboration took place on November 28, 2006, when various landless farmer, campesino, and worker organizations, including the landless movement, arrived in La Paz after marching from around the country to demand agrarian reform, and the distribution of land to landless farmers.

The MAS supported the reforms, and even encouraged the country-wide march to the senate chambers to demand the legislation, in part to give the party the excuse it needed to muscle the reforms through the opposition. Many historic marches to La Paz have taken place in Bolivia, and most have been met by military and police forces who welcomed them with tear gas and bullets. This march was different in that it was supported by the government—in fact, some marchers got bus rides closer to the capital. Events such as this march demonstrate the MAS's attempt to renegotiate its identity from that of a radical, union-built opposition social movement to that of a powerful governmental administration.

During the land reform march, I asked one woman from the Beni, a department in the north, about the possibility of police repression. "We don't have anything to worry about," she said, grabbing a coca leaf for stamina. "We are with the government now." Late at night on November 28, the marchers calling for land reform were victorious. Morales presided over the Senate—minus boycotting opposition party members—and passed the reforms while a celebratory clamor rocked La Paz.

At the time, Silvestre Saisari, then a leader in the Bolivian Landless Workers Movement (MST), said that with the MAS in power, "we feel listened to." Saisari said he saw the role of movements as one of supporting government policies that benefited the MST, and offering criticism and advice when necessary. He saw the movements' continued pressure, participation, and support as integral to the perseverance of a government that represents the needs and demands of the people. He explained, "Our democracy depends on us as social movements."[6]

A Political Instrument

The current political dynamics at play in Bolivia have much to do with the way the MAS defines itself and its goals as a party and government. The MAS administration is different from previous Bolivian governments in many ways, particularly in how it describes its relationship with the country's social movements. To find out how things operated from the MAS's perspective, and hear the party line straight from one of its key members, I met with MAS senator Gustavo Torrico in La Paz. Torrico was a stalwart MAS member and, as someone whose views reflected that of the party leadership, he frequently acted as a spokesperson to media regarding government actions. I wondered about the extent to which MAS members' view of the party was similar to that of social movements. How would Yucra's description of the MAS connect to the MAS's definition of itself?

Torrico's office in the parliamentary building lay beyond a security gate and labyrinth of hallways with walls made of tinted glass, behind which warring political parties hunkered down. We settled into comfortable chairs opposite each other in his dimly lit office. I asked him how he defined the MAS and its party structure. "The MAS is not a political party, the MAS is a political instrument," Torrico insisted. "We do not construct a political idea from top to bottom. We choose political ideas from below and move those politics upward. This is what makes us different from other parties. Social organizations are important to us because they are our essence; without social organizations, we would not exist."[7] This description mirrored Yucra's portrayal of the MAS as more of a tool for popular movements to use than an actual party.

The MAS party now had the state apparatus and was, according to Torrico, working with movements to use the state power for the people's benefit. The MAS's multiple roles and image as a social movement-based instrument and political party is part of the current dance of Bolivian politics. Indeed, the MAS has occupied these roles simultaneously.

To facilitate this connection with the movements, Torrico said the MAS representatives have meetings with movement leaders across the country every week. This offers social movements an avenue for communication in which proposals, critiques and messages regarding a range of issues, from laws and economic policies to land reform and constitutional amendments. When asked if organizations can pressure the MAS if they disagree with policy, Torrico said, "There are all types of organizations that may not agree with government proposals. So they discuss and raise these issues with their parliamentary members." He explained that things usually go smoothly because "the discussions and modifications are happening below" thanks to "a very intimate relationship with the people."

This relationship is progressive in the context of recent Bolivian history. Previous neoliberal governments rarely, if ever, met with social organizations with such goals in mind; often those past governments' relationship with movements was one based on repression, marginalization, and conflict.

Torrico and Yucra therefore consider working with the state apparatus to be a necessary element of fighting for social change. However, when the MAS party and its supporters see winning state power as the central avenue for changing society, it poses certain threats to the power of the movements. Aside from the real benefits (social programs, funding, etc.) that this relationship can produce, it does direct social movement demands into the state, thus demobilizing and corrupting often self-managed and autonomous movements, a situation in which many Bolivian movements in the next four years would find themselves.

Domesticating the Revolution

Sociologist Oscar Vega brought fresh donuts to our interview in February, 2009. The meeting took place in a La Paz apartment above a major street crowded with the city's standard demonstrations of workers demanding better wages, citizens denouncing a corrupt mayor, and MAS militants rallying in support of new government policy. This background noise seemed fitting as we ate the donuts and talked about how this vibrant civil society on the street related to the MAS government.

Vega is a long time friend and colleague of Vice-president Álvaro Garcia Linera, the academic architect of the today's MAS party. Vega is officially a government outsider but his insider's understanding of the MAS political machine often contained usefully detached insights.

Vega complemented Torrico's image of the party's relationship to movements. Various laws regarding educational, coca, and social security policies were developed, said Vega, "after many consultations with various levels of leadership among social movements that accompany the government and the constituent assembly." However,

Vega pointed out, the government's outreach efforts are essentially political. "This is the way Evo Morales can guarantee mobilization and social backing for his policies."[8]

The MAS's close relationship with movements is a two-way street; movements' goals can be met, in turn the MAS receives broad support for legislation and policies it is promoting against the will of the right-wing parties. The MAS utilizes its dominion over the movements to consolidate and perpetuate its power, and it uses the movements as its own political instruments to push new policies or mobilize during referendums, elections, and legislative initiatives that require pressure in the streets as well as in the government offices. The MAS can point to a mass mobilization as evidence that it needs to pass legislation to avoid civil unrest, even when the MAS itself has funded and organized the mobilization.

Vega pointed out that the movements in this relationship with the government can be weakened during campaign seasons for elections or referendums. When a social movement leaders participates in a campaign rather than attending meetings and assemblies with their bases, this weakens the movements' organizational capacity to pressure the government to enact progressive changes, or even to work for social change outside the realm of the state. Similarly, social movement leaders may seek positions in the government rather than work within their movements, drawing energy and focus away from the grassroots and into the government. "These same leaders are going to find themselves in a dilemma in that they permit this distance from the bases," Vega said. Just as the dance between the movements and state can have positive reciprocal effects, it can also weaken the movements and their capacity to support the MAS and its policies.

Definitions for the MAS's relations with social movements are as diverse as the country's political players. Bolivian sociologist Luis Tapia writes, "[T]he MAS is not the party of the social movements, although electorally speaking it does feed off their mobilization." Tapia believes the MAS has grown thanks to the movements, and not vice versa.[9] As the MAS took power, it reached out to movements across the country and channeled some of their energy into supporting the MAS in their legislative and electoral activities.

For a more radical critique of the relationship between the MAS and the movements, I spoke with Julieta Ojeda Marguay of Mujeres Creando, a feminist/anarchist movement based in La Paz. It was lunch time at the home of the organization, La Virgen de los Deseos, and the newest album of the Argentine band Los Fabulosos Cadillacs played on the stereo, mixing with the sounds of clanging pots and gushing water in the kitchen, where cooks prepared lunch for their restaurant.

When I met with her in early 2009, Ojeda had a critical view of the government, and was frustrated with social movements' blanket support for the MAS. "Very few organizations or movements have been critical of the MAS," she said. "The social movements have been very subordinated by the party. They won't take on a critical role. They are functionaries of the MAS and the party's interests, in part because they believe this is a process of change, and they support the MAS against the right wing. They have an empty analysis, not an oppositional role."[10]

She spoke of the strategy of some organizations to seek benefits from the government in an "I scratch your back, you'll scratch mine" relationship. Ojeda said the movements have lost sight of their earlier transformative political projects, and now just want personal benefits from the government and the party. She sees this dynamic in play when social movement leaders take on roles in government ministries, ostensibly representing their movements, but once employed by the government, needing to pursue party goals before advocating for their communities. Ojeda concluded, amid the sounds of the kitchen below, "The left hoped for more." At the same time, she admitted, neither the government nor the social movements can afford to give up any ground to the Bolivian right wing.

The fight against the right wing is another complicated dance confronting movements in the country. In spite of the contradictions and challenges of working with the government, movements know that the MAS represents their interests exponentially more than the opposition. The prospects of the right taking power are much grimmer than continuing to engage, or be subsumed by the MAS. This is one fundamental reason movements have pushed aside their critiques of the MAS and continue to mobilize in its defense. Without movements' support, it's very likely the right could have won various referendums, elections, and policy battles. The danger of right-wing success pushes people to the streets now as much as their support for MAS policies. Ironically, in a desperate attempt to prevent opposition victory of any kind, movements now collaborate with the MAS to such an extent that they are playing the same party-politics game they decried before the MAS took power.

But not everyone has warmed up to the MAS. Felipe Quispe, a long time leftist and indigenous leader, and Felix Patzi, a radical sociologist and former minister of education in the MAS government, had other visions for change which didn't depend entirely on the political party. Their views are shared by a significant, but relatively isolated number of political activists in the country. In November of 2007, the two men gave a presentation in a hotel lobby near the central Plaza Murillo in La Paz.

A mustachioed Quispe, simultaneously smoking a cigarette and chewing coca, tilted his hat above his forehead and shook his fist in the air when talking about indigenous mobilizations in recent years. "We have tried to recuperate our land and our power. Yet this power is in the hands of our looters, including the MAS. We have to reorganize, rearticulate our forces in the countryside and in the cities," Quispe boomed to the packed audience. "Who will make the revolution for us? It's us, the poor, those on the bottom, the discriminated, the workers, we who built this country, it's up to us. We need to govern ourselves." However appealing this political analysis sounds, it has been less common among mainstream political debates since the MAS took power.

The academic Patzi spoke of the social and indigenous movements that were very active in recent years and helped pave the way to the election of Morales. Patzi sees movements as still powerful in their ability to wield or rescind their support for the MAS: "The MAS is a part of the momentum of these social movements... If this movement is to go forward, it's up to us. We'll have to continue this process with or without Evo." In spite of Patzi's hopes, movements in the country have often moved forward by lining up behind Morales, cither in his party's defense, to support a policy or demand something from the government.

Yet as the sociologist Tapia pointed out at another event during that same month, "In Bolivia, politics are a lot more diverse than just the state," and it is as important for analysts as it is for movements not to wear state blinders when looking at political participation. He gave examples of communitarian governance among indigenous groups, unions, anti-privatization movements, and neighborhood councils, which question the vast inequalities in the country. "This political diversity and power often doesn't fit into political parties or governmental positions. Democracy is not synonymous with the state." He likened presidents to monarchs—both in centralized positions of power that facilitate the application of policies that can be harmful to the people—and said there is a dire need to "de-monopolize" politics and democracy in Bolivia.

The MAS party line is that their "political instrument" is opening up the political process to a wider array of people, but it's doing so with the state apparatus as its primary tool, and in some cases coopting the social movements in the effort. The party's hands may have been tied as soon as it won the presidency, occupied the state, and began to feed off the social mobilizations in the country, endangering the movements' autonomy and momentum.

Oscar Olivera, a key leader and spokesman in the Cochabamba Water War in 2000, has also taken a critical stance in regard to the MAS now that it's in power. He believes the party has worked to demobilize the movements in an effort to "domesticate them to function in the government's interests. There is a strong expropriation on the part of the state apparatus of the capacities that we have recuperated with much sacrifice—capacities to rebel, to mobilize, to organize and propose." Olivera says that those who stand in the MAS government's way, in a critical position on the left, are pushed aside, stigmatized, and labeled as allies of the right.[11]

The social movements' constrictive position of having to defend the MAS against the right wing is a common one in Bolivia, as well as in other countries throughout the world where a left-leaning party is in power. It's a typical position movements find themselves in because the argument for defense is compelling; that if the right takes over, it would be much worse. But, according to Uruguayan analyst Raúl Zibechi, that same argument is inflated by those occupying the state, who seek to subordinate movements and redirect their momentum away from autonomous emancipation. In Bolivia, he writes, "The state wants to use the right as an excuse to domesticate the rebelliousness of those from below."[12]

Autonomous Alliances

One cold evening in La Paz, a day before the March 13, 2009 anniversary of the historic siege of the city led by indigenous rebels Tupac Katari and Bartolina Sisa in 1781, I met with the writer and activist Patricia Costas at a café just around the block from the presidential palace. Costas, a long-time activist in Bolivia's Indymedia collective, co-authored a definitive book on the country's social movements with Garcia Linera before he became vice-president and was still active in academia and journalism. Due to these experiences outside the government and among social movements as an activist and researcher, she had an interesting perspective on the MAS. Perhaps even more relevant to her analysis was the fact that she worked in the government herself at the time, in the Ministry of Coordination with Social Movements and Civil Society.

Costas began working in the ministry in 2007 and was initially surprised when social organizations came to the government to align themselves as allies of the president, but also offering "a critique of the bureaucratic apparatus of the state." Costas told me that many movement representatives came to her office to say, "'the government is our government, but the state apparatus is screwing us.'"[13]

This illustrates another problem of movements' dance with the state: the Bolivian state simply doesn't work much of the time. Previous governments' mechanisms of administration via nepotism, corruption, and neoliberalism meant that the MAS stepped into a broken government infrastructure when it took power. The Bolivian state is bogged down with endless bureaucratic processes and steps that make appeals to the government an expensive and time-consuming nightmare, pushing many Bolivians to strike, protest, and go on hunger strikes for attention to their demands. The problems associated with bureaucracy in Bolivia constrain how smoothly the MAS can work with social movements, and often aggravates would-be allies, drawing them away from their families, work, and commitments to the movements they belong to.

Costas' ministry tries to ensure that demands from social movements arrive at the corresponding offices. The ministry also focuses on preventing, monitoring, and mediating social conflicts, as well as empowering and educating groups on issues relevant to their organizations. The intention itself is a clean break with the approach of previous governments. In fact, before the MAS took power, the work of her office was coordinated directly with police and intelligence officials—meaning that ministry actions were inherently reactions to tension, conflict, and violence, rather than prevention, resolution, and addressing social movements' demands.

Costas was adamant that the movements were not in positions of subordination to the MAS, and that they had largely maintained their autonomy defending their own rights and interests, as well as those of the government—when they considered it strategic to do so. She gave the following examples of such strategy and autonomy.

In September of 2008, just weeks after a recall vote invigorated Morales with 67 percent support across the country, a small group of thugs hired by the right-wing opposition led a wave of violent attacks on Morales supporters. The worst of these days of right wing road blockades, protests, and racist attacks took place on September 11, in the tropical state of Pando. A private militia allegedly funded by the opposition governor, Leopoldo Fernández, fired on a thousand unarmed pro-Morales men, women, and children marching toward the state's capital. The attack left numerous people dead and wounded.[14]

Leading up to the September 11 conflict in Pando, the city of Santa Cruz saw a high level of right-wing violence; indigenous people were attacked by violent youth organizations, media and human rights organizations were broken into and set on fire, and a string of protests and road blockades enforced by thug intimidation took place. On September 10, a working class neighborhood called Plan 3000 was hit particularly hard by this violence. Right-wing thugs entered the neighborhood, attacking the locals. But the locals resisted and were eventually successful in driving the attackers out of the area.

This wave of national violence, with its focal point in the city of Santa Cruz, and its most tragic manifestation in Pando, were deplored by leftist and pro-MAS social movements across the country. As a response to this violence, pro-MAS movements and organizations mobilized from around Bolivia, marching and traveling to Santa Cruz to lay siege to the city by blocking its surrounding highways. Approximately 30,000 people participated in the siege, in addition to the tens of thousands mobilized within Plan 3000.

Junior, a young activist in Plan 3000, reflected on this uprising's autonomy:

> People began to realize that the political leaders of the Movement Toward Socialism (MAS) have no influence on this resistance, that there was no structured leadership except for the people themselves. Nor was there logistical support from the government or from the MAS. The combatants themselves brought their own things: water, food, and sticks, and the community in an act of solidarity gave support with water, guns, and things like that. The people actually overwhelmed the MAS, overtook it, and many were questioning the fact that the MAS devotes its time in politicking but not in being with the people, because the action of the masses is what will determine political change.[15]

However, national movement leaders and those at the siege were worried about a direct confrontation between the movements surrounding Santa Cruz and the right-wing groups and thugs inside the city. There was also concern that confrontation with right-wing organizations in Santa Cruz wasn't as important as mobilizing to defend the constitution's fate, which was being decided in La Paz at the time. Cocalero leader Julio Salazar said, "Personally, I think that it would be better to pressure Congress so as to avoid confrontations between Bolivians with a siege on Santa Cruz."[16] Movement leaders pledged instead to direct energy toward organizing a siege of the Congress to pressure right-wing leaders into approving the new constitution. While many movements were prepared for maintaining a siege of Santa Cruz, and confronting the right, the leaders convinced them to remain mobilized, but change direction, Costas recounts. "Suddenly," she said, "there were 100,000 people marching toward La Paz."

The goal of the march was to put pressure on lawmakers to approve a referendum on the new constitution, and before the marchers arrived in the capital on October 20, parliament responded to their pressure and passed the referendum law. Bolivian reporter Franz Chávez recalled the diverse march weaving toward La Paz from across the country:

> Typical indigenous sheep-wool hats, multicolored caps, and ponchos from the western highlands mixed with the light clothing and straw hats of people from Bolivia's warmer eastern zones as they walked along the straight highway that crosses Bolivia's extensive altiplano, where the asphalt burns during the day but temperatures drop below zero at night.[17]

Costas participated in the march and remembered how difficult it was without water and basic necessities. But, she said, the people continued. "No matter how much capacity to organize you had, how could you take care of [all of those] people with water and food!" She said that, in spite of all of the necessities lacking, and in spite of the fact that these people were for the government's new constitution, there was no financial support from the government for the march; it was totally autonomously-organized and carried out in defense of the new constitution and against the violent right wing.

After a march that lasted nearly a week, a historic multitude of hundreds of thousands of people arrived in La Paz on October 20, 2008. The arrival in the city turned into a celebration as the Congress passed the law allowing a referendum to take place to approve the draft of the country's new constitution. The city was also flooded with a huge wave of people entering into La Paz from El Alto.[18]

These momentous events underscore the dynamic and complex dance between movements and the MAS. In this case, the right was beaten back in a coordinated effort, united by a common enemy. As we will see, the eventual passage of the constitution and electoral defeats for the right produced some bittersweet victories for the grassroots. While the fight in this constitutional battleground raged on, a different kind of battle continued in El Alto.

El Alto Changes

During the Gas War in 2003, the people of El Alto demonstrated their capacity to self-organize, shut down not only their city but the city of La Paz below with street barricades, defend the population against the military and police, topple a repressive government, and reject the neoliberal plan to export Bolivian gas. It was a monumental struggle against incredible odds. Much of El Alto's revolutionary power in various neighborhood and labor movements has its roots in the rural indigenous communities and mining unions. As part of the ongoing exodus from mining towns and rural areas to the city, El Alto's population has boomed in recent decades. This migration has brought with it solidarity, organizing skills, and an ability to revolt that has manifested itself in powerful ways since the turn of the century.

Now, with the MAS in the government, the movements' power, momentum, and solidarity have diminished for a number of reasons. To find out more about the situation among the neighborhood councils (FEJUVEs) in El Alto under the MAS government, I met with Pablo Mamani, an Aymaran sociologist and professor at the Public University of El Alto. The neighborhood councils played a vital role during the 2003 Gas War, so the participation of their members now serves as an important indicator of the current state of social movements in the city.

Mamani, the foremost expert on the neighborhood councils in El Alto, and I had met a number of times over the years in the city, discussing the themes he touches on in his various books on the subject. His expertise is particularly helpful when he dissects the evolution of the revolt in this city during the 2003 Gas War. This time when I met him, however, his assessment of the situation among the neighborhood councils was far less hopeful than it had been just two years earlier.

Mamani noted a "deficit of social leadership" among the city's leading organizations. Following the events of Gas War, the city's leaders and movement members faced cooptation, clientelism, and corruption.[19] In turn, he said, the people are not forcefully demanding of the government what they want and need. "There are unpaved avenues, dark streets, areas without water, garbage, lack of health centers, and systems of citizen security—[solutions to all of] which could be well planned between the barrios and the government, a government for the society. But these things are not being demanded." Mamani blamed the movements themselves for becoming apathetic once "their" party won power.

Part of the problem Mamani identified has to do with the structural dilemma of channeling social demands and goals through the state. Movements organized autonomously and created forms of self-governance before the MAS took power. If the party now directs those energies toward the state, it contributes to a level of demobilization.

Mamani did not believe it was the time to pressure the government in the way the city's social movements had in the past, when explicitly neoliberal regimes were in power, with road blockades and protests. Instead, he believed it was a time for "intelligent use of the negotiating table" with the government. He said that such relations would rely in part on the city's ability to pressure the government. But he was discouraged by the lack of civil participation now that the MAS was in power. "Nothing is put forward, nothing is designed, there is no dialogue, nothing is proposed." He believed the city hadn't moved forward much since the Gas War of 2003. "There has been lethargy. We need to get moving again," he explained; if the neighborhood organizations don't act, "they will be left out."

If El Alto had lost something of its protagonist and autonomous nature under the MAS, the neighborhood councils themselves were a good measure of that. Alongside one of the most congested highways in Bolivia, in the center of El Alto, I climbed the stairs of the neighborhood council office to meet with Ismael Herrera Lovera, the president of neighborhood councils of El Alto at the time. Lovera was just returning to his office from a lunch break, and dressed in the leather jacket that seemed to be standard for leftist leaders in the city. In contrast to Mamani's call for forceful participation at the negotiating table, the president of the neighborhood councils was less polite.

"We don't belong to the MAS," he said, in opposition to Senator Torrico's description of the MAS as a party made up of movements.

If the neighborhood councils, the most radical and active organizations in the country's recent history, were not part of the MAS, where did that leave the party? Lovera continued, "But we have supported the current process of structural, social, and political change in the country." He went on to say that in a city as big as this, and that is growing so rapidly, many of the water, roads, and sewage infrastructures residents need still don't exist. "And because of this, we demand attention from our authorities, and we expect to be listened to." Given the sacrifices El Alto has made in its contributions to the current process of change, the government hasn't given the city enough attention and support, Lovera believed. "But when we seriously make a proposal," he tapped his finger hard on the table, "they had better listen to us."[20]

This theme of the need to put forth demands on the government was emphasized by Mamani and Lovera. But a long-time journalist and union leader in El Alto, Julio Mamani (no relation to Pablo), provided other reasons for why El Alto is less mobilized under the MAS than in the past. He maintains that movement leaders work for proximity to power, money, handouts, and positions within the party structure and government. Therefore, when the MAS took power, many social movement leaders saw their moment to land a good job within the party.

Mamani has had his finger on the pulse of the city during the years that I've known him. As a journalist, he speaks to people from across El Alto's various neighborhoods and organizations, and as a union leader and member, he regularly attends meetings and is privy to inside information that is often kept within union ranks.

His analysis of the situation in El Alto, and the relationship between movements and the MAS was sobering. He believed social movement leaders across the city, and the country, were ignoring their bases and instead focusing on ways to gain more political power, money, and privileges, usually through their relationship with the MAS. Now that a relative ally was in power, the spoils of political victory were being sought after by union and movement leaders throughout El Alto. "These leaders are turning their backs on their bases. Meanwhile the problems of the city continue," he said. "I am not saying we should return to the times of neoliberalism, but I am making a comparison to the past, and it wasn't the same then."[21]

But according to Mamani, this dynamic wasn't just happening during campaigns and elections. He said movement leaders continued participating, just not within their own movements. People were seeking better jobs, and more money in the government now, instead of focusing on meeting the demands of their bases. "This all has far reaching repercussions into the MAS party as well, and has a national effect," he said. When leaders from any level are far from their base or constituents, this lends itself to corruption. "Over time," Mamani said, "the fact that demands aren't rising up from below because they are blocked by corrupt leaders could be devastating."

And yet, this tends to be the nature of the state, which doesn't enable ideas to simply percolate naturally to the top, as Senator Torrico claimed, but which imposes direction and policy on coopted movements that are then used as part of a political machine to simply maintain centralized power and churn out votes. The horizontal organization of the neighborhood councils has run counter to that process, but it is now in direct conflict with state hegemony in more complex ways than before.

Morales's position as the central leader throughout this entire process posed further problems, said Mamani. "It's part of an old strategy," a strategy based on "the adoration of single figure. This has happened with other political parties and leaders throughout Bolivian history," he said. "Now, it's Morales, and the problem is that the support he's given is not critical, it's just idolatry. People consider him sacred without seeing his defects. Their critical points of view are lost. It's now a mortal sin to even speak against Evo Morales." Morales as a central, charismatic figure may work within the state apparatus in creating a brand to win elections, but it also undermines democracy rather than expanding it. "It's always this way with power," Mamani said. "It's a strategy of silencing people, of making sure they don't shake the ground beneath a figure of power, of making sure they don't weaken you. These are some of the forms governments use to remain in power."

As we discussed the grim state of the neighborhood councils in El Alto, and the challenges of this relationship with the government in the MAS era, enthusiasm for the new constitution was palpable in La Paz in the period leading up to its official passage in a national vote on January 25, 2009.

Rhetoric and Action

La Paz was unusually quiet the day the constitution was passed. As driving is prohibited on referendum and election days to prevent people from voting more than once, the standard screech of bus horns was replaced with the sounds of birds singing and kids playing soccer in the empty streets. In a working-class neighborhood outside the city's center, Juan Carlos Flores, a shoe-shiner with the standard ski mask over his face, said, "I support the new constitution because it's not like the earlier ones. Now we have changes for everyone, not just for the rich." Juan Jose Arce, a MAS supporter who operates public cell phones for calls made in the street, said: "We are poor people, and we hope the new constitution will be in favor of all poor people."

That night, moments after the passage of the constitution was officially announced, thousands gathered to celebrate in the central Plaza Murillo in La Paz. Fireworks were lit at the end of Morales's speech in the plaza, sending pigeons flying. Standing on the balcony of the presidential palace, President Morales addressed the raucous crowd: "Here begins a new Bolivia. Here we begin to reach true equality." The event was underscored by the fact that just over fifty years ago, indigenous people were prohibited from entering that same plaza. Cheers and horns sounded off sporadically across La Paz. Morales said: "I want you to know something, the colonial state ends here. Internal colonialism and external colonialism ends here. Sisters and brothers, neoliberalism ends here too." But neoliberalism did not really end with the passage of the new constitution; it just took on a different mask. In this case the mask was the populist rhetoric of the MAS party and its leader.

As the night wore on, people began dancing to bands playing folk music in the street. At midnight, when the police asked the thousands gathered to leave the plaza, the crowd marched off, taking the fiesta to central La Paz, cheering nearly every Latin American revolutionary cheer, pounding drums, and sharing beer. After marching down a number of blocks on the empty streets, the crowd settled down for a party at the base of a statue of none other than Latin American independence leader Simón Bolívar.

The demand for a new constitution was one that preceded the MAS's time in power. Bolivia had sixteen constitutions leading up to this one. The nation was one of the first South American countries to rebel against Spanish rule, and, in 1825, finally won independence. When Bolivia's first constitution was drafted in 1826 by Bolívar, he stated that the country would "be known as an independent nation."[22] The constitution passed in 2009 under the MAS was similar in its lofty rhetoric and historical implications.

Many Bolivians saw assurances in the text of the new constitution that would give them greater rights and access to legal recourse for injustice. Among other significant changes, the new constitution created space for a broader involvement of the state in the Bolivian economy, including the state's participation in the gas and oil industry. The document calls for broader access to basic services, education, and healthcare, and prohibits US military bases on Bolivian soil. It establishes the Bolivian state as a pluri-national entity to reflect the diversity of indigenous and Afro-Bolivian groups in the country. It formally promotes the official use of the country's thirty-six indigenous languages. The new constitution also grants autonomy to indigenous groups across the nation, enabling them to govern their own communities, and expands the number of seats in the recently opposition-controlled Senate, and specifically reserves other seats for senators elected from indigenous communities.

Under a law created by the new constitution, land deemed productive will not be broken up by the government, but unproductive land will be redistributed, and a cap on new land purchases set at 5,000 hectares. Land reform is an area of the constitution that was highly criticized from the Bolivian left. Critics said the constitution should have gone further in addressing the fact that most of Bolivia's land is in the hands of just a few wealthy families. These weak land reforms are considered a major concession to the right wing; much of Bolivia's fertile land is in the eastern departments, currently controlled by opposition prefects. The changes don't necessarily leave the realm of global capitalism, but at least on paper, they enshrine many of the changes a large sector of the population hoped to see.

The conflict surrounding the constitution not only defined Morales's first years in office, it galvanized social movements and the right wing into joining a party-based battle over the future of the country. The constituent assembly became a stage where much of the country's tensions and conflicts played out, from the election of political party representatives as assemblypersons in 2006, to actual physical conflicts within the assembly in 2007, and finally the social movements that mobilized toward its passage in 2008 and 2009. The document itself represented both the radical forces shaping the country from the grassroots on up, as well as the reformist tendencies among the MAS to concede to an economically and politically powerful but marginalized right wing.

Though the writing of a new constitution was framed and initiated as part of a struggle for self-determination, indigenous rights, de-colonization, and more, it was largely reduced to a battle between the right and left parties in Bolivia. Party politics dominated the assembly from the start, as candidates for assemblypersons had to be affiliated with a political party in order to run, leaving those outside of parties out of the central debate. Julieta Ojeda of Mujeres Creando echoed this concern, "In order to participate, people had to lend themselves to a political party. A better way would have been allowing social organizations and movements to participate directly by running candidates for election... This would have given the assembly and constitution much greater legitimacy."

The right in Bolivia is widely represented in political parties, whereas the left and social movements have tended to operate more through unions, and have been more excluded in the political arena in recent years, with the exception of the MAS. By limiting participation in the constituent assembly to just party members, the assembly marginalized some of the country's most representative and politically popular sectors. It also effectively channeled dissent and political power on the left through the MAS in the assembly, helping the party to monopolize the debate. In part because of this organizational issue, the constitution became a kind of referendum on the MAS, and a symbol of defiance against opposition parties. Many Bolivians felt they had to back the version of the constitution supported by the MAS against enemies on the right.

Most of the enthusiasm I heard from more critical Bolivians was a thankfulness that at least the constitution hadn't been defeated, because otherwise it would have been a political victory for the right, adding to their campaign fodder against Morales. There was a lot to celebrate, but in terms of the dance between the state and the movements this proved to be less of a victory for the people of Bolivia than a victory for the MAS. Indeed, much of the content of the constitution may remain on paper and never be acted out in reality.

Yet hope lies in the fact that the movements and people could run with the radical promises of the constitution, demanding and enacting changes themselves, just as people did during Bolivia's Revolution of 1952. At that time, campesinos demanded land through occupation, and the government was therefore obligated to expropriate the land and grant it to them. In that case, the government was only formally recognizing an expropriation the people had already made.

Patricia Costas of the Ministry of Coordination with Social Movements and Civil Society believes there are important similarities between the politically charged period of 1952 and today. Costas explained:

> Various landless movements in Bolivia have said "Okay, now we have the new law, this law was created in December of 2006, and what is needed? To execute it!" This is the logic, which is simple, and they continue occupying land. And the government is trying to slow this down, on the one hand saying it won't permit illegal occupations, but on the other hand it says we have to comply with the law.

In this way, the people push the government, radicalizing MAS policies from below. Within the dance between the state and the movements in Bolivia, the constitution creates important new political space for the grassroots to flex its muscles.

Aymaran sociologist Pablo Mamani said, "The challenge is how to put these philosophical, theoretical, and rhetorical ideas from the new constitution into practice." Moving the changes from paper into reality has been an obstacle for numerous constitutions throughout Bolivian history. Perhaps now, with the MAS in power, and the movements pushing for radical change, a combination of forces will unite to create changes that will indeed help the country's impoverished majority in the short and long term. To what extent movements may be coopted or lose autonomy within this process is still to be determined.

In the meantime, Carlos Arce, an economist and political analyst from the Research Center for Labor and Agrarian Development in La Paz, said that there is a gray area within the constitution. It is unclear, for example, how much land could be granted to whom, or where money from the gas industry could be directed. According to Arce, this vagueness could enable social movements to fight for interpretations that favor their communities. Social organizations could take that opportunity to demand land or money for their town. People could, as Costas pointed out, not wait for the bureaucratic process of land redistribution to take its course but take over land themselves.[23]

"There is an effect of the discourse of the MAS, which is a radical discourse," Arce explained. "But the MAS wants calm. It wants to win the presidential elections and stay in power for another five years, or another twenty years. But the people will react based on their own necessities." He believes that "[a] new stage may develop in which people say 'this constitution recognizes us, it gives a priority to our rights,' such as defining access to water as a human right. This same discourse, however limited, could reactivate the people and provide a good motive for mobilization. It could also strengthen some social movements to make their own demands a reality."

But even that is a compromise; why should the people require the state to give them what is naturally theirs to begin with? If the movements truly lead the government, then the MAS would be made peripheral in the struggle for liberation. That is not the course that Bolivia is currently on. Yet recent history shows that the future of Bolivia is certainly hard to predict. While the country continues to dance with Evo Morales and the MAS party, new challenges and opportunities will inevitably emerge. The future of the country will depend on how the movements navigate a rocky road filled with nepotism, corruption, and cooptation, and how well they can rise above party politics and the adoration of a single leader.[24]

Bolivia is not the only Andean country involved in such a precarious dance. Throughout the MAS's rise to power and time in office, indigenous movements in Ecuador fought to transform their country in a parallel vein. This nation to the north is similar to Bolivia in its geography, dependence on hydrocarbons, passage of a new constitution, and indigenous culture. Ecuadorian indigenous movements would face new opportunities and challenges with the 2006 election of left-leaning president Rafael Correa.

Participants in a march against neoliberalism in Quito, Ecuador during the second Social Forum of the Americas in July 2004. Photo by: Patricio Realpe/ANPE

CHAPTER TWO

Ecuador: Indigenous Uprisings and Betrayals of the State

When the Ecuadorian government passed a law enabling the wholesale transfer of indigenous land to oil companies in 1994, indigenous groups mobilized across the country. One of the road blockades was constructed by activists along a major highway from the Andes into the Amazon. An eyewitness described it as a "long, red tarp stretched across a narrow, one lane bridge straddling El Topo River." The indigenous activists "braced themselves against the wind, cold, and rain in defense of their lands."[1]

In fact, for many, this was a last opportunity to save their communities. As Magdalena, an indigenous participant in the blockade, said, "I am ready to spill my blood for our territory. At least my gravestone will say that I died fighting in 1994." In response to the blockade, the president had road blockades and protesters cleared off the streets by tanks and soldiers.[2]

At a negotiation meeting following the conflict, the president told indigenous leaders, "Don't you waste my time—the time of a president who has many other important issues to attend to!" To this, indigenous leader Nina Pacari replied, in a reference to the initial colonization of latin America by Europeans, "We have 'wasted' more than 500 years of our time."[3]

When Rafael Correa took office in January of 2007, the brutal battle that the country's indigenous people fought against the government took on new dimensions. Following his election, Correa moved forward on campaign promises, including the creation of an assembly to rewrite the country's constitution, using oil wealth for national development, and confronting US imperialism. However, once the electoral confetti stopped falling, the Correa administration began to betray the indigenous movements' trust on many fronts. The dynamics playing out in Ecuador offer distinctive insights into the relationship between social movements and the state.

The nature of the indigenous movement's dance with the Ecuadorian state grows from the history of the country's oil, a contentious resource that has been mostly a curse for the Ecuadorian people and environment. The Amazon River Basin stretches across various countries and is home to the biggest rainforest in the world. In eastern Ecuador, 32 million acres of tropical rainforest support vast biodiversity, as well as numerous endangered species and indigenous peoples. Over a dozen self-defined indigenous nations live within the borders of Ecuador, making up to 40 percent of the country's population. Many fled to this area to escape slavery during the rubber boom of the late nineteenth and early twentieth centuries.[4]

But avoiding one threat, indigenous people faced another: the oil industry. This booming industry has directly attacked the autonomy and livelihoods of indigenous communities. The Shell Oil Corporation began operations in the region in the 1920s. The new roads it created led to a wave of missionaries and new settlers on the land. Texaco-Gulf found oil in the Amazonian rainforest at Lago Agrio in 1967, and set up hundreds of miles of pipelines in the following years. Over two dozen foreign oil companies followed, generating a vast oil transportation infrastructure that stretches throughout the Amazon and beyond.[5]

This oil boom didn't benefit the impoverished majority of the country at all. In fact, the number of people living in poverty rose dramatically throughout this period. Often, any money that flowed into the Amazon was from oil corporations and went to pipelines rather than social programs or necessary infrastructure. In some cases, indigenous tribes disappeared entirely. Working with governments friendly to foreign corporations and dismissive of indigenous rights, oil companies operated in an environment of near impunity, with no responsibility to the people living in areas where they drilled and refined oil. Over the years, the companies' waste and spills created sickness in local communities, destroyed indigenous cultures through displacement, and devastated the environment.[6]

As development sociologist William Waters notes, "If you've been to the Amazon, you'll see that despite some small improvements in paving roads, it is like going to another world. All the resources go out and very little goes in."[7] Yet to this day, the oil industry is a central part of Ecuador's economy, often directing economic policy. Forty percent of Ecuador's export income comes from oil, and it is the second biggest importer of oil to the US from South America after Venezuela.[8]

The indigenous territories that the oil industry overlaps onto are considered autonomous by various indigenous groups. Indigenous leader Luis Macas explained this concept of indigenous land:

> Territory involves not only the concept of market, the concept of development, and the concept of production, but also the funda-mentally spiritual concept of territory in the indigenous world. We are part of nature. We are part of the land, of territory, in such a way that, in this context, if we do not have this fundamental ele-ment we are not able to speak of education, of health, of identity.[9]

Such autonomy, organization, and vision have been at odds with the capitalist-driven oil industry and pro-industrial vision of twenti-eth century Ecuadorian governments. The indigenous communities of Ecuador have organized the fiercest resistance against the envi-ronmental destruction wrought by the neoliberal extractive indus-tries of oil and mining. Instead of protecting indigenous territories and rights, the state has continually used strategies of cooptation and repression of indigenous peoples to aid mining and oil compa-nies. These tactics include the intentional destruction of the envi-ronment and ecosystems that indigenous people depend on, and the imposition of forms of agriculture that exclude and displace indig-enous communities. As sociologist James Petras points out, poverty, pollution, and environmental destruction force indigenous people to leave their communities and enter the capitalist marketplace.[10] In spite of overwhelming odds, many indigenous movements and groups have risen up against this threat to the survival of their cul-ture and way of life.

Movement for Survival

A nationwide indigenous uprising shocked the racist political and corporate elite ruling the country in 1990. The activists hauled trees and boulders on to major highways, blocking transportation to cit-ies, pressuring government officials with long-unmet demands for access to bilingual education, land reform, and official recognition of indigenous territories.[11]

The tactics and actions on the part of the indigenous were widespread. In addition to road blockades and protests, the Santo Domingo Church in Quito was occupied by 160 indigenous activists demanding the resolution to land disputes; indigenous-managed food markets shut down and food supplies from indigenous areas were blocked, both showing the national reliance on indigenous food production. The government responded with harsh crackdowns, deploying military, police, tanks, and tear gas. The uprising was organized and led by the Confederation of Indigenous Nationalities of Ecuador (CONAIE). While the revolt shocked politicians, it established the indigenous movement as a major political and social force.[12]

CONAIE was founded in 1986 by various indigenous leaders and communities to advocate for indigenous rights, access to land, autonomy, basic services, environmental protection, and political representation. The indigenous participants who made up the backbone of CONAIE were largely poor and believed the economic and political system in the country aimed explicitly to destroy indigenous culture, enrich corporations, concentrate power, and marginalize the poor majority. CONAIE sought to subvert and transform this anti-democratic and repressive society.[13]

From its beginning, CONAIE was a very grassroots organization with dispersed local bases that met to debate and make decisions collectively. Regional and national meetings continue to take place today, making major decisions about national campaigns, actions, and elections.[14] The democratic nature of CONAIE has been useful in dealing with repressive and non-cooperative governments. The direct participation of the local chapters helps to hold movement leaders and representatives accountable, and the strengthening of a cohesive indigenous identity has spurred unity within the movement.

A 1992 statement from CONAIE illustrates the organization's distinction within the national terrain of Ecuadorian movements, setting it apart from traditional union structures and working toward political "methods that faithfully reflect our own manner of arriving at consensus. The base organizations make decisions and the leadership of CONAIE serves as an intermediary between those decisions and the actions taken."[15]

The organization of CONAIE is based on decentralized, local communities, in part because of the isolation and self-sufficiency of rural areas. The structure of the organization allows for quick mobilization to set up road blockades, celebrations, or projects that improve the communities. This capacity is facilitated by easily-accessed communication and collaboration between the decentralized grassroots base of the organization, located in small indigenous communities across the country, and the elected leaders within the organization at regional and national levels. Over the decades of its existence, CONAIE has ignited and sustained numerous campaigns and actions thanks to this organizational structure.[16]

CONAIE has utilized various tactics to achieve its goals including protests, marches, discussions with government officials, and involvement in elections and campaigns.[17] The usefulness of the movement's political tool box was demonstrated in its flexibility and capacity to change with the political environment. CONAIE's history proves that drawing from such tactics involves an unsteady dance with the government, and a need to constantly re-evaluate strategies.

Several uprisings related to land and oil issues in the early 1990s are illustrative of CONAIE's power and strategies. In April of 1992, CONAIE members from around Ecuador marched to Quito in a call for land reform. Coinciding with the five hundredth anniversary of Columbus' arrival to the Americas, the protest demanded that indigenous lands be recognized and that Ecuador officially become a pluri-national state: a state of many nations, officially recognizing the diversity of indigenous nations in the country, rather than a single nation-state. Five thousand strong by the time they arrived in Quito, the marchers delegated one hundred people to enter the palace to meet with the president. While the march established the indigenous organization as a powerful political force to contend with, the government's concessions were literally superficial. The president gave them titles to roughly half the land they demanded, and then only to the land's surface: the state continued to legally own and control the subsoil, and said that any activity that blocked oil operations would be deemed illegal.[18]

The state also divided the land to pit indigenous groups against one another, opened the land up to oil exploitation, granted military access to certain areas near the Peruvian border, and extended the boundaries of the country's national parks—all of which limited indigenous activity. This was but one of many conflicts in which the government turned its back on indigenous people.

In spite of such setbacks, the movement kept up its fight. The ability of CONAIE to continue mobilizing in the face of such state repression and institutional racism speaks to the organization's momentum, cohesion, and size. Its success, in the long run, was also based on its ability to retreat, regroup, and rehabilitate following defeats in negotiations with the government. Such tactics would prove useful in the following years, particularly in a precarious dance CONAIE entered with the administration of Lucio Gutiérrez in the early 2000s.

Divergences

As part of CONAIE's strategy of defending its autonomy as a grassroots movement, for many years it did not get involved in electoral campaigns or endorse candidates.[19] This policy came to an end, however, in 1996, when the Pachakutik political party was formed as an extension of CONAIE. Though CONAIE remained officially autonomous from Pachakutik, the party did allow the movement in general to direct its discontent and demands more effectively into the governmental arena.[20] CONAIE's new relationship with electoral politics would ultimately have devastating consequences.

Before entering the next electoral challenge, however, sectors of the indigenous movement played a role in a short-lived coup. Military colonel Lucio Gutiérrez helped lead the coup in 2000, which ousted then President Jamil Mahuad, who had been responsible for initiating the dollarization of Ecuador's economy. As a result of the dollarization, many of the prices of basic foods and goods rose dramatically, sparking protests. A coalition of military, indigenous, and labor leaders took power in the short-lived coup which ended after President Bill Clinton and the US embassy successfully urged the Ecuadorian military to intervene. Previous vice-president Gustavo Noboa then took office, and Gutiérrez was kicked out of the military and sent to jail for six months. Upon leaving prison, the former military man and coup leader hopped on the 2002 presidential campaign trail.[21]

In the 2002 presidential race, Pachakutik and CONAIE allied themselves with presidential candidate Gutiérrez. Their popular support was pivotal to his eventual victory, as it expanded his narrow voter base to include rural voters across the country. In return, Pachakutik leaders were awarded ministerial positions in the government under the Gutiérrez administration. Gutiérrez's election was seen as the first of its kind in Ecuador: a military man coming to power through democratic means, rather than through a coup. Largely due to his alliance with Pachakutik, Gutiérrez's election was seen as something of a victory for the left. However, the pact with leftist sectors did not add up to much: once in office, Gutiérrez sought alliances with the country's elite, watering down his commitments to CONAIE and Pachakutik.[22]

After taking office on January 20, 2003, Gutiérrez signed an agreement with the IMF that effectively dismissed his promises to indigenous groups. He appointed neoliberals and members of the ruling elite as ministers—further demonstrating that Pachakutik and other leftist allies didn't have a say in the formation of the government. His administration then went ahead with the privatization of various sectors of oil, electric, and telecommunications industries. Gutiérrez worked against the labor movements protesting the privatizations, firing, jailing, and generally harassing union leaders, particularly those in the oil sector. The social base of the indigenous and leftist movement was outraged.[23]

After just three months in office, Pachakutik and CONAIE broke ties with Gutiérrez, leaving their government posts and withdrawing support. However, the alliance with Gutiérrez had already tainted the indigenous party and movement.[24] In a 2008 interview, CONAIE President Marlon Santi spoke of the relationship with the Gutiérrez administration, when

> the State intervened directly to break CONAIE's unity, because the Indigenous movement has a historical base and is a constant threat to the government when we propose territorial autonomies,

the handling of our natural resources in their own territorial dis-
tricts, when Indigenous nationalities manage their own biodiversity—all this is a danger to each government and transnational
interests.[25]

However, CONAIE strategically survived the political crisis by
retreating from the political scene, moving away from its alliances
with Gutiérrez back to its bases where it reinforced its grassroots
direction and democratic decision-making processes.[26] This strategy
was adept, and unfortunately based on hard-earned experience: various social movements in the country had long suffered a carrot-and-
stick mixture of cooptation and repression in their relationships with
several governments.

Gutiérrez would leave the political arena almost as dramatically
as he had entered. On April 15, 2005, he declared a state of emergency to quell protests against his unilateral dismissal of the Supreme
Court. Tens of thousands of activists—including many members of
CONAIE—marched through the streets of Quito. The crackdown
further upset protesters, and unrest continued to rock the city.[27] On
April 20, Gutiérrez was forced from office by both the protests and
a vote by Congress to replace him with Vice-president Alfredo Pala-
cio. In the wake of these events, CONAIE faced the question of how
to participate in the upcoming 2006 presidential elections.

In a new strategy, counter to its history as a movement, not a
political party, CONAIE decided to run its own presidential candidate, Luis Macas—who was also the president of CONAIE at the
time. In a 2006 interview, Macas spoke of his organization's strategy following the betrayal of Gutiérrez. As a way to rehabilitate the
movement after the Gutiérrez debacle, the movement considered the
elections as a step that would "maintain and strengthen this recon-
struction of the indigenous movement." The tactic of entering the
campaign was in part about movement-building and participating in
the electoral process by bringing indigenous issues and demands into
the national electoral debate.[28] Macas said, "We are not in these elections to win. We won with Gutiérrez and where did that leave us?
The country is worse off than ever! We are in this because we are
constructing a solid process from the roots, a political project with

our own hands, using our own minds. This is how we will advance. It doesn't matter if we win or lose."[29]

This strategy was complicated by the candidacy of Rafael Correa, a self-defined progressive with a populist rhetoric and strong nationalist policy platforms that mirrored those of Hugo Chávez in Venezuela and Evo Morales in Bolivia. The dangerous combination of hope and betrayal that defined his candidacy, and eventual election, has led to a period of Ecuadorian politics rife with contradictions and conflict.

Weakening Dissent

On the campaign trail, Rafael Correa promised to fight against neoliberal economic policies, the marginalization of indigenous people, US imperialism, and environmental destruction. All were seminal issues that CONAIE had been organizing around for years. Yet following the betrayal of Guiterrez, CONAIE and Pachakutik were wary of an alliance with Correa. Therefore, when Correa offered the position of vice-president to Pachakutik in exchange for the party's support, Pachakutik declined, in part because it was running Macas as its own presidential candidate. Part of Macas' hesitancy to join Correa was based on the bitter memory of Gutiérrez. "First of all, we don't know who Rafael Correa really is," said Macas. "Just like we didn't know who Lucio Gutiérrez really was."[30]

As the campaign went on, their position changed. CONAIE and other movements decided to support Correa in the second round of votes as he faced right-wing candidate Álvaro Noboa.[31] Again, the logic of the political party and campaign based around winning state power through elections was at odds with the goals and strategies of movements. In an electoral compromise that has occurred again and again in other South American nations, the more radical approach of a progressive movement and party was undermined by the need to support a "lesser of two evils."

While this support helped Correa defeat the right, CONAIE's initial wariness was warranted: Correa turned his back on the indigenous people and Ecuadorian left almost immediately upon taking office. Though some relatively "progressive" policies were enacted, his administration continued and even expanded aspects of the neoliberal agenda. He worked perhaps even harder than previous governments to crush the indigenous movement and anyone who stood in the way of the government's plan for privatization of natural resources, and the expansion of mining and oil industries.

In spite of such betrayals, Correa's electoral victory was also largely a victory against Plan Colombia's US-led war on drugs, the old Ecuadorian oligarchy, US-style free trade deals, and electoral fraud.[32] In October of 2007, Correa announced that his administration would not renew Washington's lease on a US airbase in Manta, Ecuador, unless Washington allowed Ecuador to open a military base in Miami: the US refused and was thus forced to leave Manta. Correa began an audit to see which sections of Ecuador's debt should be written off as illegitimate under international law.[33] The result was the announcement that Ecuador would not pay $9.937 billion in debt, roughly 19 percent of Ecuador's GDP, because the debt commission he appointed concluded that the debt had been accrued illegally by past undemocratic governments, including a dictatorship from 1974 to 1979.[34]

A more controversial change under Correa was the convening of a constituent assembly to rewrite the constitution, responding to a decades-old demand from indigenous movements. Macas explained that this demand from the indigenous movement was based on a desire for official recognition of the various indigenous nations in the country. They demanded that the state become pluri-national to reflect the diversity of indigenous land and customs. This process was seen as more than just changes on paper. The transformation Macas and others sought had to do with structurally changing the state itself. Macas explained that the Ecuadorian state is a state

characterized by a lot of exclusion of these [indigenous] sectors. There hasn't been any integration of people for almost 180 years of the republic's life—a vertical state, a state that legislates, a state that, in other words, hasn't arrived for all these social sectors. We believe that the character of the state must be pluri-national, a state that recognizes each one of the existing nationalities in this country.[35]

This transformation, of course, never happened in the constitutional assembly under Correa.

From the beginning of Correa's proposal to change the constitution, many members of the indigenous movement considered the constituent assembly itself as undemocratic. For example, like Morales in Bolivia, Correa looked to political parties, not movements, to participate in the assembly, and social movement representatives were not invited to be part of the commission that formed proposals for the new constitution. This all limited the transformative role the constituent assembly could have had.[36]

Following the work of the assembly, the rewritten constitution was passed by 64 percent of voters on September 28, 2008. Many Ecuadorians supported the new constitution as a tool to ensure lasting institutional and social change. The document was progressive in the sense that it expanded state regulation and involvement in the economy and management of natural resources, recognized the rights of nature, and the human right to an education and healthcare. But many such changes have been undermined by Correa's emphasis on the extractive industry's potential benefits for the state—in spite of environmental and territorial concerns by the indigenous.[37] The president forged ahead with oil and mining concessions that ignored the rights of indigenous communities. In many cases, such concessions were given by the state without consultation with the indigenous communities the extraction would most affect.[38]

Correa's approach to the constitution was emblematic of the way he dealt with other pressing issues relating to indigenous demands. In the first years of his presidency, instead of working toward renewable alternatives to oil, Correa sought to expand this industry, as well as the mining sector, in order to generate funds for government programs and initiatives. As part of this strategy, Correa has silenced opponents to his mining policies including the environmentalist group Acción Ecológica. Author and journalist Naomi Klein characterized the government's decision to shut down this organization as "something all too familiar: a state seemingly using its power to weaken dissent."[39]

CONAIE has not been immune to such crackdowns. Economist, professor, and former advisor to CONAIE, Pablo Dávalos noted that Correa has benefited and expanded upon past government strategies of weakening CONAIE, particularly following their destructive relationship with Gutiérrez. He said that Correa uses strategies that "neutralize the ability of the indigenous movement to mobilize and to destroy it as a historic social actor."[40] By pushing CONAIE out of the political debate and calling on police repression to crack down on their dissent, Correa has worked to undermine the indigenous movement.

Such views were also reflected by indigenous activist Monica Chuji who worked as an assembly member in the constituent assembly as part of Correa's party. Chuji believed Correa not only assimilated CONAIE's radical discourse into his administration, but drew from the momentum of movements pushing for certain policies, only to then block much-needed change. Correa has utilized Ecuador's legacy of grassroots uprisings and movements for his own political ends, Chuji said. "Correa's regime has capitalized off of all of this. He has collected this accumulation of historic social and political demands" and is "usurping this [political] capital." She gave the example of how social movements had been pushing for a new constitution for years but Correa took that initiative, and then curtailed its transformative potential by limiting assembly people to political parties and, once it was written, signing legislation that undermined the rights it gave to indigenous communities.[41]

A War Continues

Another disappointment for the social movements that supported Correa has been his administration's repression of leftist activists and the criminalization of dissent. One of the first signs that Correa would use serious force against leftist protests came with a conflict in the Amazonian town of Dayuma in November of 2007. Protesters were opposing an oil company's activity in the region by setting up roadblocks to prevent access to oil fields. They called for the government to improve their community's standard of living and infrastructure, rather than prioritizing the needs of multinational oil companies. Correa responded by declaring a state of emergency. Police violently dragged community members from their homes, arresting twenty-three people. In a similar move, on July 8, 2008, police arrested ten activists who were protesting the construction of a hydroelectric dam on a river near their community and had occupied land near it for six months.[42]

Movements found themselves in a tricky position, forced either to support Correa as the lesser of two evils, or oppose him and risk fueling the right's power. As Ivonne Ramos of Acción Ecologica explained, "There is the question of public sympathy, which is complicated when you have a president with such high approval ratings. Any action that a social movement takes can be read, understood, or publicized as an action in support of the Right, since this government is supposedly a Leftist one. This has produced a climate of uncertainty over what positions to take, what actions to take."[43]

On May 12, 2008 CONAIE decided what action to take: it officially broke ties with the Correa administration. This rupture focused specifically on their frustration with the failure of the new constitution—under Correa's watch—to recognize Ecuador as a pluri-national state. CONAIE also protested the lack of changes in the constitution to require that communities to be impacted by extractive industries must provide their consent before those industries proceed with operations. The CONAIE statement asserted:

> We reject President Rafael Correa's racist, authoritarian, and anti-democratic statements, which violate the rights of [indigenous] nationalities and peoples enshrined in international conventions and treaties. This constitutes an attack against the construction of a pluri-national and intercultural democracy in Ecuador. Correa has assumed the traditional neoliberal posture of the rightist oligarchy.[44]

The conflicts that emerged during Correa's time in office show his administration's higher interest in defending the rights of multinational corporations and environmentally destructive policies, rather than in defending the rights of the impoverished majority of his country.

His administration also rushed ahead with large scale extraction projects and privatization of natural resources. On January 29, 2009, the Ecuadorian government passed a mining law which doesn't allow for community members to participate in discussions about how the extraction will proceed, and paves the way for widespread water and environmental pollution.[45]

Correa's government has also proposed laws that CONAIE says will lead to the privatization of water in their country, limit community participation in the management of water, and lessen punishment for water pollution.[46] The launch of the National Mobilization to Defend the Water in September of 2009 saw protesters marching throughout the country, setting up road blockades with burning tires, rocks, and logs on major highways. CONAIE leaders said they were pushed to this action as they were "exhausted by the process of dialogue."[47] Protester Ceaser Quilumbaquin said, "We are indigenous people and the majority of water comes from our páramos [plateaus]. Water is life, and the government wants to sell water to private entities."[48] At the time of this writing, the fate of the controversial water law is still undecided.[49]

In spite of such conflicts, Correa was re-elected president with 52 percent of the vote on April 26, 2009, in part due to his continued populist rhetoric and heavy social spending. His re-election was historic in the sense that it was the first time since 1979 that a candidate received enough votes to prevent a run off election, which requires 50 percent of the votes, or 40 percent with a 10 percent lead ahead of the nearest opponent.[50] While his re-election signaled a further defeat for the Ecuadorian political establishment and right wing, it presented new challenges to the indigenous movement.

On September 30, 2009, just months after this landslide victory at the polls, two indigenous protesters were killed and dozens injured in a conflict between indigenous communities and police forces regarding the proposed water law. Indigenous leader Tito Puenchir denounced the violence, explaining that the "dictatorial president Rafael Correa has declared a civil war against the indigenous nationalities of the Ecuadorian Amazon."[51] Correa has perpetuated a state-based war on the region's indigenous that is over five hundred years in the making.

The story of CONAIE's rise as a major political force in Ecuador, its subsequent relations with political parties and electoral politics, and the current repression and marginalization it faces from the Correa administration shows that CONAIE as a force of dissent is not naturally welcome into the sphere of the state or within the realm of dominant political parties. It is in a party or ruling president's nature to conserve and centralize power, not disperse it, or engage oppositional political forces. CONAIE presents a radically transformative agenda that would make Correa, the state that benefits from his neoliberal policies, and the corporations that continue to destroy the Amazon, powerless and irrelevant. It is no surprise then, that Correa turned his back on the indigenous movement.

Decades after the emergence of CONAIE as a national movement, their demands and tactics are as timely as ever. The survival of the movement under Correa relies on its ability to understand this complex terrain, know the stakes of their dance with the state, and defend their own autonomy, both through pressuring the state and empowering their own territories from below.

Workers from the self-managed cooperative Hotel BAUEN rally for an expropriation law. Photo by: Marie Trigona

CHAPTER THREE
Argentina: The Rebellion and the Ballot Box

M en in business suits had hollow stares as they walked down the streets of Buenos Aires, Argentina. Women wearing expensive jewelry could not afford lunch in the restaurants they passed. Streams of smoke from roadblock bonfires regularly mixed with the downtown exhaust. Supermarkets shelves were empty and the glass windows of banks were smashed from ongoing protests.

Almost overnight in late 2001, Argentina went from having one of the strongest economies in South America to one of the weakest. During this economic crash, the financial system collapsed like a house of cards and banks shut their doors. Faced with such immediate economic strife and unemployment, many Argentines banded together to create a new society out of the wreckage of the old. Poverty, homelessness, and unemployment were countered with barter systems, factory occupations, community soup kitchens, and alternative currency. Neighborhood assemblies provided solidarity and support in communities across the country.

"The revolution began because people had no work," Paloma of the Palermo Viejo neighborhood assembly said. People were pushed together by class-blind suffering and a widespread outrage at the institutions and politicians that led to the crisis. "The unemployed, in particular, reached a point where they said, okay, we organize or we'll die. It was a question of survival. I think they discovered that they had nothing, and they had no one to trust except themselves."[1] This awareness was a key building block of the horizontal organizations, grassroots institutions, and exchanges that emerged.

One march on January 28, 2002, in which the people went from La Matanza to the Plaza de Mayo in Buenos Aires, reflected this unity. According to one account of the mobilization, "Breaking old class prejudices, women from apartment buildings joined young people from poor neighborhoods, marginalized families, semi-literate people stood under the sun with the families of professionals dressed in suits and ties."² This exuberant climate of mutual aid fused with a creativity born of crisis and need.

In 2003, Nestor Kirchner was elected president of Argentina, and began a precarious dance with these movements. His policies, "progressive" in some areas, were also aimed at coopting, dividing, and demobilizing the dynamic movements. The strategies of the Kirchner administration, combined with other factors, successfully undermined the energy of the movements, in many cases redirecting the momentum arising from the crash into electoral politics and the government.

More Bullets than Ballots

Many of the movements that came to the forefront in the 2001 uprising in Argentina had their roots in resistance to the dictatorship that lasted from 1976 to 1983, a harsh experience that still casts a shadow across generations of Argentines. "During the twentieth century, we have more governments in Argentina elected by bullets than by ballots," noted Argentine investigative journalist Horacio Verbitsky. He was referring in part to the so-called "Dirty War," the popular name for the period of state violence perpetrated by the military junta led by Jorge Videla. In order to implement the neoliberal model, the dictatorship needed to crackdown on those involved in radical movements. At the start of the crackdown, one of the generals in the junta predicted, "We are going to have to kill 50,000 people: 25,000 subversives, 20,000 sympathizers, and we will make 5,000 mistakes." By the time the dictatorship fell approximately 30,000 people were forcefully "disappeared."

Much of the state violence had been carried out in secret, but in 1997 Argentine Lieutenant Commander Adolfo Scilingo confessed to participating in the torture and murder of political prisoners during the Dirty War.³ These activities included "death flights"—drugging prisoners and then throwing them, alive, out of airplanes into the ocean. In other cases, torturers used cattle prods and pulled toenails off their victims.

The right-wing paranoia spread throughout society; high school teachers in the 1970s and 1980s reported unruly students to the government, and leftists buried their literature in backyard gardens. Many Argentines are still searching for family members—both parents and children—who were abducted and have never been found.

The dictatorship's violations of human rights ended with the return to democracy in 1983. But as time wore on, workers faced new challenges: forms of repression that weren't wielded through the barrel of a gun or the electric prod of a torturer, but through economic policy. Following the end of the dictatorship, Raul Alfonsín was elected president. His economic policies continued those of the junta; many of the dictatorship's economic and financial officials remained in their governmental posts.

Under the Videla regime, Argentine subsidiaries of companies such as IBM Argentina, CitiBank, Bank of America, Renault, and others had been encouraged to go into debt. The Alfonsín government paid off these companies' debts with taxpayers' money. In order to rid the government of the burden of continuing to administer public utilities and services, Carlos Menem, Alfonsín's neoliberal successor, proceeded to privatize everything in sight, selling most of the country's state-run companies and resources at low prices to foreign buyers. In order to combat inflation, the Argentine government set up an economic plan in 1991 that pegged each peso to the US dollar. This allowed the government to distribute only pesos that were backed in the reserves by dollars.[4]

Menem's privatization of public assets and services, combined with deregulation of private industry, deindustrialization of Argentine industries, and free capital flow, effectively destroyed the Argentine government's control over its own economy. Most of the country's domestic banks ended up in the hands of foreign companies, who favored lending to their traditional multinational corporate clients rather than small and medium Argentine businesses. This stunted national growth considerably. At the same time, the International Monetary Fund (IMF) pushed for cutbacks in social spending and increased taxes, hitting the middle class hard, increasing the deficit, and spinning the country out of control.[5]

Meanwhile, the government's debt grew at a rapid rate, from $8 billion in 1976 to nearly $160 billion in 2001. This forced the government to spend a disproportionate percent of tax revenues on loans and interest, instead of maintaining social programs, education, and health care.[6] Though the effects of these policies were devastating to Argentina's working class, people organized a resistance during this period that would form the backbone of the transformative social movements that haunted the Argentine elite and changed the direction of the country.

Growing Out of the Wreckage

While the social movements that emerged in the wake of the 2001 crisis formed rapidly, many of their concepts and actions came from pre-existing movements. In the crash of 2002, the Argentine economy hit rock bottom, but the boat had been sinking for decades, and some passengers had been building lifeboats.

Neoliberalism undermined the base from which many workers were organized. There were fewer factories employing people due to deindustrialization. Closed factories meant losses for unions which had taken decades to form. Many of the jobless had been previously employed in public energy and service industries privatized by Menem. Thus was born the piquetero movement which drew from waves of unemployed workers.[7]

Piqueteros—the name is based on the word *piquete* (picket or road blockade)—hit the streets together to demand work and social assistance. This movement set itself apart from the dominant Peronist labor movements and federations in which workers called for better conditions and salaries, partly because the older movements had been repressed extensively under the dictatorship, and because economics were changing the country, forcing social movements to change with it.[8] With previous movements weakened by neoliberalism, the piqueteros rose up from the wreckage of the 1990s as a formidable force in 2001.

Unemployed workers embraced the tactic of blocking roads to direct attention to their demands. Blockades pressured powerful sectors in an effective strategy after other routes of negotiation, such as dialogue with the government or standard protests and public rallies, were exhausted. The blockade made piquetero demands visible, and gave the movement a point of leverage for negotiations. The

frequency of the blockades in the 1990s spoke of worker desperation and the popularity of the tactic during a period when unemployment rose to over 20 percent: in the span of 1997 alone there were
seventy-seven blockades across Argentina.[9] However, piquetero proposals, demands, and tactics were far from capturing the support of
middle-class Argentines, who weren't in such desperate situations as
the piqueteros—yet.[10]

In December 2001, the neoliberal party ended. A heavily
indebted Argentine economy was blindsided when scared investors
catching rumors of the impending crash pulled $140 billion out of
the country. Argentina defaulted on $100 billion of debt and the
banking system crashed. In early December, to slow the run on
banks, the government limited the amount of money people could
take out of their bank accounts, and then converted private pen-
sion funds into government bonds to pay back the debt to the IMF.
Argentines who went to the bank found the doors chained. Middle
class people became poor, the poor went hungry, and unemployment skyrocketed, reaching 20 percent by December 13.[11] Tens of
thousands of all ages and socio-economic strata hit the streets in
protests. Social upheaval rocked the country and the government
declared martial law on December 19. Police repression left over
twenty dead.[12]

Middle class Argentina woke to find itself broke and hungry,
with a lot more in common with the piqueteros. A larger sector of
the population was now desperate and willing to try activist alternatives and tactics previously seen as too radical. A shared sense
of rage at the political establishment pushed people together; they
united under the cry "Que Se Vayan Todos!" ("Throw them all out.")
Political turmoil in the streets and Congress led the country to go
through five presidents in two weeks. Congress finally agreed upon
Eduardo Duhalde as the president.[13]

During this uprising, emerging social movements saw a need
for piquetero skills. "The radical piqueteros ... deployed their well-
honed tactic of erecting road blockades. But they also helped launch
cooperative efforts to run bakeries, kitchens, schools, construction
teams, and libraries," writes journalist Mark Engler.[14] It was these
activities, coupled with factory occupations and neighborhood

assemblies that made the social activism in Argentina in 2002 so impressive, concentrated, and creative.[15]

The framework for mutual aid demonstrated by piqueteros was taken up by larger sectors of society when the crisis hit. A wide cross section of people traversing class lines saw that the political system was not working for them. They embraced radical alternatives out of a need to survive as the economic crisis pushed people together.

Occupying a New World

Other groups of workers and activists besides the piqueteros altered the political landscape as well. Perhaps the most well known responses to the economic meltdown in 2001 were the occupations of factories and businesses, which were later run collectively by workers. There are roughly two hundred worker-run factories and businesses in Argentina, most of which started in the midst of the 2001 crisis. Fifteen thousand people work in these cooperatives and the businesses range from car part producers to rubber balloon factories.

"For workers in Argentina there is no law. It only exists for the powerful," said Eduardo Murua, president of the National Movement of Reclaimed Companies (MNER). "If we were stuck outside [of the factory] asking the judge to keep it open, we would get nowhere. If we were to ask politicians, we'd get even less. Only through occupation could we recover the jobs."[16] Workers across the country were driven to occupation out of political principle as well as need.

Occupation sped up a legal process in Argentina which worked in the workers' favor in many cases during the crisis. The legal steps were already in place for workers to take over bankrupt factories and businesses. The actual transfer could take place after the owners declared bankruptcy, faced lawsuits from creditors, or left their business due the weight of debt. If the workers take over at this point, they maintain the right to operate the business. Often, the owner continued to own the business, but the workers had the legal right to operate it. In some cases, workers rented the space and equipment from the owner, and in others, the government expropriated the bankrupt business and gave it to the workers who had a certain period of time to pay for the equipment.[17]

Luis Caro, a lawyer who has advised workers who take over businesses in Argentina, said it is very important that this legal process exists in Argentina for workers to take over businesses that have closed: "We have been able to get many judges to agree that when the destiny of the society is in the balance, private property should come after the right to work."[18]

Such was the case with Sime Quarry, located in Victoria in the province of Entre Rios. The owners of the quarry ran the business into the ground, leaving its employees without jobs. But the quarry was eventually taken over by the workers and kept in operation under worker control. Leading up to the closure, the bosses had been abusing the workers verbally and physically. María del Huerto, forty-five years old, said that in December of 2002, the bosses of the quarry gave workers a thirty-five-day "unscheduled vacation." The "vacation" lasted until January 20, when the workers went back to the quarry to find it abandoned. It was "a pasture with no lights, running water, or telephone service. Nothing. It was desolate," María said. Just a few machines were left; the rest had been sold off by the owners in an attempt to make a few more bucks off the bankrupt factory before they fled.[19]

Realizing that they had been fired without severance pay, María met with fellow workers and members of the MNER, and discussed taking over the quarry themselves. They decided to arm themselves before the takeover just in case they ran into any resistance. "We took firearms, and some neighbors lent us shotguns. We announced that we didn't want to shoot anyone, but wanted to defend our workplace and keep the bosses from stealing anything else."[20]

It was a terribly hot time of the year, mosquitoes were everywhere, and no one had any money—so workers used the guns to hunt for food during the occupation. "To eat, the men hunted apereá rabbits—they're brown; they look like big mice. They also fished caruchas from a nearby lagoon, and Don Joaquín would send us tarpon fish from the market. What had happened to us? We thought of ourselves as middle class, and here we were, begging and hunting to make ends meet," María recounted. At one point, the workers were so desperate they had to sell furniture in order to buy meat. Over time, they discovered that the bosses of the quarry had been evading taxes, strengthening the legal argument for worker control. The workers formed a cooperative and a judge ordered the plant be given over to them in April 2003. The workers now have the quarry in operation, and are fully functioning as a cooperative.[21]

A similar story played out in a factory on the outskirts of Mendoza, Argentina. In the worn-out meeting room of another of Argentina's worker-run factories—Cerámica de Cuyo—Manuel Rojas ran a rough hand over his face. The mechanic recalled forming the cooperative after the company boss fired the workers in 2000: "We didn't have any choice. If we didn't take over the factory we would all be in the streets. The need to work pushed us to action."[22]

Cerámica de Cuyo is surrounded by vineyards and artists' homes in the town of Bermejo. The business produces roofing tiles and bricks, and employs around thirty two people. Dust blew around the sun-baked factory yard as I sat down with Rojas and his co-worker, Francisco Avila. Rojas wore a weathered blue plaid shirt while Avila had a baseball cap resting on a head of gray hair. We were in the Cerámica de Cuyo meeting room. The ancient chairs had crumbling foam cushions. Phone numbers and Che Guevara quotes were scrawled on the walls. It was easy to sense the wear and tear that lifetimes of labor had on the place.

In August of 1999, the Cerámica de Cuyo owner cut wages. Though he promised it was only temporary, the lack of money pushed many employees to search for work elsewhere, some even heading outside the country. "The boss kept promising money, so we waited," Rojas said. "We worked on weekends, waiting and waiting, but no paychecks arrived. We had to support our families, pay the bills, and everything." Finally, they were simply fired, their back wages still unpaid.

After working at the factory for nearly thirty-five years, Rojas and the other two dozen workers at Cerámica de Cuyo began to organize into a cooperative. It wasn't easy. While organizing the cooperative after being fired in February of 2000, they had to guard the factory to prevent the previous owner from stealing expensive equipment and machinery. Neighbors helped the workers out at this critical time, providing food, firewood, and blankets. "Workers from other cooperatives came to the factory to teach classes, informing us how to organize a cooperative," Avila said. "This kind of solidarity is common."

Before the formation of the cooperative, the pay scales were typical, with the owner earning a lot more than the workers. Following the formation of the cooperative the workers decided together how to restructure pay, administration, and benefits, with everyone being paid the same amount and all workers allowed one week of vacation. Regular assemblies are now organized to discuss administrative and financial topics, or to hire a new employee. Since they formed the cooperative, they've been able to buy newer machines.

Workers are now more involved in the business of their factory, symbolically and literally. "Before, the boss wouldn't let us into the main administrative office. Now it's ours," Rojas told me. "We go in there anytime to check on orders and to be involved with that side of the business."

We walked outside into the scorching sun. One truck dumped off a load of dirt while, across the yard, clay was formed into bricks and tiles and sent inside a massive kiln. Rojas works as an all-around mechanic, fixing everything from forklifts to conveyor belts. When we entered the main factory room, he was called from three directions at once with questions to answer and problems to fix. Steam rose from the hot, wet, recently cut bricks. The whole place smelled like a potter's kiln.

While Rojas worked on a control panel for the conveyor belt, Avila took me upstairs to his work area at the top of the kiln. The temperature rose by about twenty degrees Fahrenheit. Though it felt like a sauna, Avila seemed comfortable and turned up the radio to a popular *cumbia* song. Worker control hasn't made his work easier— it's still a dangerous job: "Sometimes when the electricity is shut down, and the gas keeps going, there can be an explosion, so I have to pay attention."

In many ways, worker control demands more from each individual. "It hasn't been easy," Avila said. "Before, we were workers. Now we have to be lawyers, accountants, and everything. Before, we didn't worry about the machines. Now they're all ours, so we care more about them. Now, when a machine breaks down we have to wait for money and parts."

Both men admitted that one of the hardest things about working in a cooperative was that all workers, young and old, received the same wages. Rojas says, "Some people who have no experience at all are making the same per hour as those working as mechanics with thirty-five years of technical experience."

Avila agreed. "Some workers want to earn more for working less. At the beginning it was all *compañero* this and *compañero* that, very glorious. But when we started working more, a lot of the conflicts broke out about salaries."

Back in the meeting room, Rojas explained that now, whenever there is a problem, they all discuss things in the open, in assemblies. "There are always conflicts, but what's good about it now is that we solve it together, right here." He pounded his fist on the battered meeting table.

Workers in similar situations across the country looked to take-over their places of work and form cooperatives under worker control. These are just some of the examples of radical tactics Argentines employed, building new systems of work based on solidarity. But these pockets of resistance would come up against new challenges at the ballot box, complicating strategies, dividing movements, and channeling revolt.

A Lesser of Two Evils

On June 26, 2002, the Duhalde government attacked a piquetero road blockade at Puente Pueyrredon, a major bridge. Police used live ammunition on the protesters, killing activists Dario Santillan and Maximiliano Kosteki. Presidential elections were announced just days later, and Duhalde himself backed Nestor Kirchner as a candidate.[23] The resignation of Duhalde, whose administration called for the repression, and the announcement of the presidential election, was seen as a victory by many on the left.[24] Repression and elections contributed to pushing people out of the streets.

The momentum and energy following the 2001–2002 uprising dispersed and became less intense in the lead up to the 2003 presidential elections. Many members of movements were divided as to how and if to participate in the elections and campaigns at all. The left's main option was Kirchner, a political outsider who had served three terms as governor in the province of Santa Cruz in southern Argentina. His leading opponent was a well known entity—Carlos Menem, who, perhaps more than any other politician, had led the country into the crisis it found itself in.

Argentine analyst Ezequiel Adamovsky said Kirchner's election in 2003 was the result of people having to choose the lesser of two evils, "under the threat of the return of the neoliberal right, and in a situation in which no serious electoral alternatives were available." He believed Kirchner's economic and political policies demonstrated continuity rather than the radical changes that many movements were demanding leading up to the election. Yet Adamovsky admitted that there were important distinctions between Kirchner and the other candidates. "Menem, for example, was openly announcing severe repressive measures in his TV adverts. López Murphy, the neoliberal candidate ... would have virtually destroyed what is left of public health and education, and also repressed the social movements with no mercy."[25]

The dynamic of this election demonstrates the way electoral politics traps movements into accepting limitations on their struggle for social change. Interviewed before the election, Daniela of the Unemployed Workers' Movement [MTD] in Almirante Brown, said "Admittedly, Kirchner is no one's idea of the best solution, but he is the lesser of two evils. For us, [Kirchner]'s terrible, just terrible." But, Menem's candidacy involved a further danger. If he were elected, "the struggle would continue, but at a greater cost, because this guy would be very threatening to us." Under Menem, she predicted, "there would be more of a military presence in the streets and that would be rough on us. That would destroy more [social] organizations."[26] As in other countries, Argentine movements confronted this electoral dilemma of supporting the lesser of two evils, and, as the aftermath shows, they faced the consequences.

The "lesser of two evils" argument is quite familiar to anyone living in a capitalist economy administered by representative forms of democracy that offer electoral rather than structural or economic alternatives. However, the heightened tensions in Argentina threw certain aspects of the dilemma into stark relief. As Uruguayan analyst

Raúl Zibechi notes on this period, strategic priorities of social movements can become clearer in electoral situations:

> If the state is in danger of falling into the hands of fascist groups, we should do all we can to prevent that from happening, including participating in the elections, in a direct form or in support of other connected groups. But we know that there, in this field, in this space, what is central to our future is not being fought over. We will not put our best forces in this terrain because we know that what is fought over there, usually, is not decisive in terms of changing the system.[27]

The state, of course, did its best to redirect those forces toward the electoral arena. It was not convenient for politicians to have an empowered population that looked beyond the state to create its own world from the grassroots. "[Politicians] don't ask us anything except for our vote," Rosa, a piquetera from the Unemployed Workers' Movement in Salta, described. "The poor vote for politicians, but if we fight, they hit back hard with rubber bullets, tear gas, and sending the National Guard out."[28] Though Kirchner rode the country's discontent into the political office, promising alternatives, he was able to do so only because people's energy was redirected out of the streets, neighborhood assemblies, and road blockades, and into the ballot box.

In the end, Kirchner was elected president. And his "evil" was, in certain respects, probably "lesser" than Menem's would have been. He refused to follow the suggestions of the IMF, which recommended further cuts in social spending and a smaller role for the government in the regulation of the economy. He instead threatened to default on the country's loans if the IMF didn't back down. The strategy worked; the IMF was afraid other countries would follow Argentina's lead.[29] Many argued that Argentina should have entirely defaulted on their loans, given that the IMF and World Bank caused the crisis to begin with. However, as writer Tariq Ali explains, "Kirchner's repayment scheme of 30 cents on every dollar that it owed on the $100 billion loan has saved Argentina a great deal of money and reduced the country's indebtedness, whereas a total default could have led to sanctions."[30] Kirchner managed to bring about surprisingly fast growth with these unconventional negotiations, and with state intervention in certain areas of the economy.[31]

Under Kirchner, from 2003 to 2007 the economy grew nine percent annually, and unemployment and poverty levels dropped by approximately 50 percent during this time. Part of his popularity was based on policies that included raising the minimum wage, empowering the rights of workers and unions, and expanding social security programs to more unemployed people and workers in the informal labor sector. The funding and attention toward public services such as housing and education rose significantly. In addition, the Kirchner administration sped up the prosecution of criminals involved in the 1976–83 dictatorship.[32]

One major turning point for human rights in the country took place during Kirchner's first year as president, when he took down portraits of military dictatorship leaders Jorge Rafael Videla and Reynaldo Bignone from the wall of the National Military College. Kirchner said at a related rally, "I come to ask for forgiveness on behalf of the state for the shame of having remained silent about these atrocities during twenty years of democracy."[33] In 2005, the Argentine Supreme Court overturned rulings that granted amnesty to participants in the dictatorship; this legislative move was made possible in large part by Kirchner's replacement of certain judges on the Supreme Court who were blocking such progress.[34]

Kirchner worked with the Argentine Workers' Central (CTA), a major union, to implement a labor law that allowed them to organize for better wages. He put a limit on prices and rates set by privately-owned services that had been privatized under Menem in the 1990s. He put the previously privatized postal system under state control, started up state-run energy and airline companies, and revamped the judicial system, which had allowed for so much corruption under Menem.[35]

Given the political and economic conditions in Argentina when he was elected, one could argue that Kirchner had little choice but to make certain concessions in order to prevent even broader, and more fundamental, social transformation. He admitted that his goal was to essentially reconstruct capitalism in the country, "a capitalism in which the state plays an intelligent role, regulating, controlling, and mitigating where necessary problems that the market does not solve."[36]

This kinder, gentler capitalist economy would include a role for the state in addressing social problems, poverty, and human rights. Kirchner and his wife, Cristina Fernandez de Kirchner, who was later elected president in 2007, sought "to build a Latin American welfare state and bring about conciliation between social classes, centralizing power in the distributional state."[37] This approach brought some sectors of society back on their feet and into employment. But it also was a drastic departure from the radical experiments in direct democracy that the country had been working with at the time.

Dispersal

In spite of any policies that benefited the nation's poor, Kirchner actively worked to demobilize and divide Argentina's movements. In a comment that is reflective of the Kirchner administration's desire to re-route the grassroots fervor into institutional processes, the president called upon piqueteros to use the ballot box as a route for their demands, saying that voting was "the only concrete and legitimate way of living together that a country and modern, progressive democracies can have."[38]

Kirchner's dance with an outraged and mobilized population involved major transitions within the political debates from the streets to the government palace. "Whoever assumed the government in Argentina [at the time of the election] faced the difficult task of transforming protest into politics, of somehow institutionalizing social mobilization that was anti-institutional," says sociologist Nicolás Casullo.[39] The process of institutionalization of the movements described by Casullo manifested itself in many different ways.

First of all, Kirchner effectively demobilized and bought off the middle class. He also spread division among movements through granting subsidies to certain groups and sectors and not others. Divisions emerged internally among movement participants who were at odds regarding whether or not to support the Kirchner administration at all. Opportunism, the desire for a position in the new government, also drew movement leaders away from their bases. Kirchner resorted to outright repression of certain movements, isolating and excluding them from the public and political sphere. After applying these divisive, demobilizing, and repressive tactics, the government used the simple strategy of patience and attrition while public activism died down.

Kirchner's approach was part of a larger strategy to restore legitimacy and belief in institutions that the wide majority of society saw as illegitimate and corrupt. Under the Kirchner administration, the government used liberal economic policies to create employment and stability, but also to effectively win the support of the middle class. As Kirchner created the calm necessary for the management of the country from the presidency, the middle class largely ceased participating in protests and neighborhood assemblies. Improvements in the economy created jobs and satisfaction with the status quo, leaving many to forget the activist work they were forced into in December of 2001. The middle class' absence in activist actions and gatherings was an important development that contributed greatly to the decline in social movement activity. After Kirchner's election, the middle class, desiring a return to normalcy, called for patience and moderation. They could now afford to leave the streets and condemn protesters again as a public nuisance.

The government facilitated the decline in public participation, providing subsidies to certain groups, coopting their leaders, which resulted in less radical demands and fewer blockades. In other words, Kirchner was handing out crumbs when what many demanded was revolution.[40] This tactic reflected the administration's broader agenda, which included painting governmental policies as progressive, when in fact they saved the same bureaucratic institutions and hierarchies that many fought to destroy and overcome in the 2001 uprising.

The divisive question among many movement leaders was whether or not to support or join Kirchner in his relatively anti-imperialist and comparatively progressive government, work for some long overdue victories, or to operate outside electoral politics. Leaders of the Madres de la Plaza de Mayo threw in their support for Kirchner, as did some piquetero leaders, while others refused to join the electoral parade.[41] James Petras points out that some social movement leaders' support was based on Kirchner's "public purge of some of the more notorious military and police officials and the granting of subsidies to certain sectors of the human rights movement, including the Madres de la Plaza de Mayo."[42] Other movement leaders simply left the streets to enter government offices.[43] Journalist Jim Straub contends that Kirchner was "endeavoring to woo a minority of the Piquetero groups to his side by offering small concessions to their members and political benefits to their leaders; and to then repress, even smash, remaining groups insistent on advocating for real economic changes."[44] Such an approach physically manifested itself in certain crackdowns on road blockades and protests under Kirchner.

A government that initially portrayed itself as a friend of social movements eventually sent its police into the streets to repress its former supporters. Previously, Kirchner pledged to not repress the social movements during protests and road blockades, a clear break with the policies of earlier administrations. But as actions in the streets expanded into his time in office, he resorted to standard strategies of repression. On September 5, 2004, *El Clarín* reported that "Kirchner had issued an order [to Minister of the Interior, Aníbal Fernandez] to remove the social conflict from the streets." On September 24, the Buenos Aires City Council passed regulations allowing for harsher crackdowns on any groups impeding the flow of traffic with road blockades.[45]

Soon, militant piquetero groups, who in 2001 to 2002 enjoyed the support of the more middle class neighborhood assemblies, were again marginalized. Many of those allies from the middle class eventually called for repression of the piqueteros as the movement continued blocking roads and utilizing other protest tactics long after the worst of the crisis had passed. According to Buenos Aires-based journalist Andrés Gaudin, Kirchner's specific strategy for the piquetero movement focused on "protecting them while awaiting their natural disintegration."[46] Along with direct repression, his strategy involved the silent treatment: a selective lack of direct repression of the groups while they were protesting and blocking roads.

The Kirchner government ignored and isolated certain radical sectors of the piquetero movement in order to demobilize them.

Kirchner preferred "a strategy of wearing out the resistance," journalist Federico Schuster writes. Due to their relative lack of structure and unity, the movements proved to be unsustainable in this context.[47] "Instead of encouraging the development of these movements," Schuster explains, most leftist parties spurred on division. "This has contributed to one of the greatest problems of the piquetero movement, which has ended up exacerbating its weakness—namely, dispersal."[48] Within this fractious experience, demands became disparate, for government financial support one day, school supplies the next day. These were all signs that the movement was waning.[49]

So it was that one of the most expansive and momentous grassroots uprisings of the 21st century dissipated. Though many of the practices, groups, and acts of solidarity remain, they are shadows of what they were in 2001 and 2002. While many factors, including a middle class desire for a return to class separation, contributed to this decline, the logic of the state and political parties were particularly destructive to many of these once vibrant movements.

Yet many movements that are still active have taken important lessons from this experience. "Political parties are the most pacifying commodities," said Emilio of the Tierra del Sur neighborhood assembly, occupied building, and community center.

It's much more comfortable to vote, and to remain within the system of representative politics ... and to blame the President, than to participate in the day-to-day creative initiatives of the assembly, the piqueteros, the occupied centers and factories, indigenous communities, and other self-organized initiatives throughout Argentina. It's much more comfortable to complain and vote, and to vote and complain.[50]

But many groups and movements across Argentina and South America continue to act autonomously, creating new worlds on their own terms.

This cycle has repeated itself in uprisings and revolutions throughout history, and modern day South America is no exception. Case studies throughout the region demonstrate that the challenges confronting grassroots movements are diverse and formidable.

Identifying, understanding, and knowingly confronting—or avoid-ing—these obstacles are key aspects to overcoming them. From the piqueteros in the 1990s to the more contemporary cooptation of the Kirchner administration, the successes and defeats of Argentine movements provide many lessons for social movements that want to continue to exist beyond the confines of the electoral process.

Throughout this period, comparable challenges and opportuni-ties faced Uruguay, right across the Rio de la Plata from Buenos Aires. This country was hit by the same crisis that pummeled Argentina, and its citizens responded in similar ways. The next chapter looks at the long road of Uruguay's Frente Amplio party, and the intersection of electoral and grassroots forces that make up the country's unique political landscape.

A celebration in Montevideo, Uruguay marking the two year anniversary of the Tabaré Vázquez presidency, in 2007. Photo by: Sílvia Leindecker

CHAPTER FOUR
Turning Activists into Voters in Uruguay

The smell of fried food and sausage sandwiches filled the Montevideo air as José "Pepe" Mujica assumed the presidency of Uruguay in March 2010. Street vendors lined the inauguration parade route selling Uruguayan flags to the boisterous crowd which cheered, "Olé, olé, olé, Pepe, Pepe." Mujica, a former member of the 1960s–70s leftist Tupamaro guerrilla movement who was imprisoned and tortured under the country's dictatorship, stood in front of the multitude with his wife and vice-president as he led the crowd in singing folksongs outlawed during military rule.[1] Uruguayan writer Eduardo Galeano, who was himself exiled during the dictatorship, said the period opening up with the inauguration of Mujica "is born blessed with the enthusiasm of the people, the fervent hope of the people, and this is something to take care of, to be very careful to not defraud. It is a day of celebration but also of compromise."[2]

Mujica lives with his wife outside the city on a farm where he grows vegetables and flowers. María del Rosario Corbo, a forty-four-year-old neighbor of Mujica, spoke of the new president, "He's just an ordinary guy: you see him on his bike, his motorcycle, working among his flowers... He's going to strengthen the focus on the poor, giving them a helping hand."[3] However charismatic and popular Mujica is, he owes a lot to the Frente Amplio (Broad Front), a political party that over the nearly forty years of its existence has transformed the political and social landscape of the country. The intersection between Uruguayan social movements, grassroots groups, and institutions linked to the Frente Amplio, and the machinery of the party itself offers insights into the contradictions and victories that have marked the party's long road to the presidency.

The Frente Amplio's Long Road

The Frente Amplio (FA) began as a broad coalition of leftists that pulled together the Christian Democrat, Socialist, and Communist parties of the country in 1971. The FA created an initial campaign plan that reflected the policies of socialist Chilean President Salvador Allende. The platforms called "The First Thirty Government Measures" was revolutionary at the time, calling for transformative agrarian reform, state control of private banks and other businesses, and a stronger government intervention in the national economy and foreign trade.[4]

The FA began with incredible odds against them, not the least of which was the challenge of breaking through the country's two party system. Starting in 1830 when Uruguay officially won its independence from Spain, to 2004, the country's politics were dominated by two right-wing political parties: the National Party and the Colorado Party.[5] While the FA posed a threat to this monopoly on political power, it wouldn't successfully threaten it on the presidential campaign trail for over three decades after its formation.

But from the very beginning, the FA had a wider scope than just the presidency. The FA founders said the "fundamental objective of Frente Amplio is permanent political action and not electoral competition." As part of that plan, the FA began nation-wide networks of grassroots base committees to open up the political process. Through these committees, they aimed to create a space and culture of direct democracy from below, with fewer political intermediaries, and grassroots power over decisions within the FA as a movement.[6]

From the grassroots level of the base committee, participants raised issues to higher coordinating levels within the party. A fundamental aspect of this dispersed network was to provide a forum for debate within the party. As FA senator and former Tupamaro leader Eleuterio Fernández Huidobro put it, "When the FA was created the idea of the base committee sprouted up to allow us all to speak straight from the soul."[7] Though these committees operated within the confines of the political party, they did provide vital outlets for discussion, politicization, building solidarity and awareness, and encouraging activism in broader movements.

The coalition faced widespread repression under the dictatorship which began in 1973. Many leaders of the party, including Mujica himself, were imprisoned and tortured during this period. The FA reemerged as a political force after a return to democracy in 1984, and the Uruguayan left and the FA's base committees continued to grow throughout the late 1980s.[8] However, after making it through the dictatorship, the party and Uruguayan activists in general faced new challenges. For the Uruguayan left, repercussions from the dictatorship, as well as the growing neoliberal pressures on state and social institutions made solidarity and activism necessary for survival. Uruguayans came together through these struggles, strengthening their capacity to mobilize and developing successful grassroots and campaign tactics. This political activism benefited both the population in general and the FA.

The Uruguayan left leapt into action in 1986, when Congress passed the Law of Impunity, a measure proposed by the administration of Colorado Party President Julio María Sanguinetti to protect the former dictatorship's functionaries from prosecution.[9] Many people united against this affront to the human rights movement, participating in a referendum to get rid of the law. Twenty-five percent of voters' signatures were needed to convoke the referendum. Uruguayan analyst Raúl Zibechi writes that, to make sure the referendum was passed,

> neighborhood activists combed the country, going house-to-house, to dialogue with neighbors and explain what the law was about and to ask for their signatures. Some 30,000 activists participated in the door-to-door campaign. They visited 80 percent of Uruguay's households; spoke with over one million people; and in some cases had to return two, three, and even seven times to obtain a signature.[10]

The referendum failed—42 percent were against the law, 52 percent were for it—partially because of the fear that those responsible for the military crimes would retaliate. However, it led many activists to become more familiar with their country's political climate and fellow citizens, and allowed for a stronger presence in rural areas. This heightened political awareness and aided in the electoral advances of the Uruguayan left.[11]

The use of referendums in Uruguay has been a widely popular method of democratizing politics and decision-making in the country. Uruguay holds the record for conducting the most referendums in the western hemisphere in the twentieth century.[12] From referendums on human rights legislation to the management of water and state industries, the practice has played a major part in policy development and social movement building. Uruguayan social scientist Alicia Lissidini said referendums have helped "force the political elites to debate issues that they might otherwise prefer not to address." An essential part of the referendums is popular participation, such that referendums in Uruguay have been supported by politicians "only after the issue has been raised by social movements."[13]

The political momentum of the 1980s resulted, in part, in the election of FA outsider Tabaré Vázquez as the mayor of Montevideo in 1989. Though he ran as a member of the FA, he did not rise up from the party's grassroots base. This worked to his benefit in some ways during the race; because he hadn't participated in the FA during the dictatorship, a politically broad cross-section of voters viewed him as a relatively neutral leader. That said, as an FA mayor, his policies and stances reflected many of the party's key goals and principles.[14] When Vázquez entered the mayoral office in 1990, he established a broad network of organizations and methods to encourage people to participate in local government.[15] Neighborhood councils were designed to actively monitor government operations and participate in budget-making, as well as to design social projects and consider laws and policies at the grassroots level.[16]

Another event that empowered the Uruguayan left was a 1992 referendum over a neoliberal law proposed by President Luis Alberto Lacalle of the Nationalist Party that would have privatized the national telephone company and other publicly-run services. Such policies echoed the standard mixtures of privatization and deregulation that were popular among many South American presidents during the 1990s. The referendum politicized people, spread awareness, and galvanized movements and unions against the legislation. As a result, 72 percent of the population voted against the law.[17]

The transition from the dictatorship to a more typical representative democracy would enter a new phase in the early 2000s with the onset of a devastating economic crisis and a political window of opportunity for the FA. How the party's base would participate and react to these events would play a key role in the FA's electoral success.

Crisis and Opportunity

Uruguay is right across the Rio de la Plata from Argentina, and is tied politically, economically, and culturally to what happens in its comparatively larger, more populated, and economically powerful neighbor to the south. The two countries are further intertwined through the fact that many Argentines keep their money in the relatively more stable Uruguayan banks. Banking is one of Uruguay's major industries, aside from agriculture and tourism. In 2002, this industry took a major hit, with the poorest Uruguayans paying the highest price.

In July of 2002, Uruguay's currency value dropped dramatically after the government blocked access to bank accounts in an effort to prevent a widespread run on banks. Leading up to the move, Uruguayans and Argentines fearing the devaluation of their money withdrew millions of dollars—33 percent of total deposits in the country—further crippling the Uruguayan financial system which still hadn't recovered from the impact of the crash in Argentina. Similar to Argentina, Uruguayan citizens arriving at banks to withdraw money found their accounts frozen.[18]

Some of the citizens confronting economic trouble joined the FA base committees as outlets for activism. Oscar Gandolo, a painter in Montevideo, told me, "The economy was going from bad to worse. I had to do something." So he joined one of the committees. "We have meetings every week where we get together and decide what we think the government needs to do, and cover issues that the government misses." This space for political participation, provided by the FA, was in direct opposition to the way politics were run by the two dominant political parties.[19]

Uruguay's crisis was tied to neoliberal policies that favored privatization, prioritized national debt payment over public well-being, and led to larger deregulation of the economy and banking sector. Such policies were applied by then Colorado President Jorge Batlle and his right-wing predecessors. Though popular protest in Uruguay did not reach the height it did in Argentina, anger directed at the established parties and political institutions was similarly widespread.

One manifestation of this discontent included the voting down of privatization measures in a 2003 referendum. A broad-based coalition of movements, social organizations, and groups organized the National Commission in Defense of Water and Life (CNDAV) to fight water privatization. The CNDAV gathered hundreds of thousands of signatures in October 2003 for the following year's plebiscite, which took place along with the national elections. Over 62 percent of the people voted for a constitutional change to prohibit the privatization of the water and sewage systems.[20] The CNDAV offers another example of how a mobilized population can overcome neoliberal policies through broad-based campaigns and activism. In confronting the privatization of public services, water, and sewage systems, activists went outside party politics to work for change.

Further eroding the population's trust in the Colorado Party, the Batlle administration developed close ties to US President George W. Bush. Batlle supported the war in Iraq in spite of the fact that 90% of Uruguayans opposed the war. He also okayed sending "peacekeeping" troops to Haiti and supported the continuation of the US embargo against Cuba. Guillermo Stirling, the Interior Minister under Batlle, was chosen as the Colorado's candidate against the FA's Vázquez.[21] Given the deterioration of the incumbent party's public image, it was a politically ripe time for the FA to focus on the presidential race. Furthermore, the party's socialistic platforms appealed to a wider variety of voters following the 2002 economic crisis.

Vázquez was the FA's likely candidate for the presidency due to his prominent position and popularity as mayor of the country's largest city. The 2002 economic crisis, discontent with the ruling parties, and desire for alternatives to neoliberal policies, gave former mayor turned presidential candidate Vázquez leverage for pushing his platform of "change." However, the extent to which Vázquez was seriously going to confront the neoliberal agenda was a moot point; he was the most formidable candidate against the failed politics and economics of the Uruguayan right. His electoral promises, the legacy of his party, and the hope he embodied compared to the country's nightmarish years under the dictatorship, were enough to convince the population that change was in the air.[22]

The base committees and the privatization referendum helped lay the framework for the FA's popularity, support, and campaign networks, which led to Vázquez's election to the presidency. On the campaign trail, Vázquez promised to prioritize policies to fight marginalization and poverty, expand healthcare and education services, and increase democratic participation in the development of government policies. Yet as election day neared, he was willing to water down the FA party principles and plans he had supported as a mayor in order to expand his voter base. Although the FA leadership distanced itself from its historically radical politics, it still harnessed much of the party's grassroots energy to bring about an electoral victory.

At this time, José Mujica was gaining popularity as a strong figure in the FA, and he spoke of his party's plans before the 2004 elections that would make him a Minister of Agriculture. Unlike the party's radical agenda of the past, Mujica said he did not believe the FA would come into office "on the crest of a revolutionary wave. We are almost asking permission from the bourgeoisie to let ourselves in." He continued, "I sincerely believe that we have many things to do before socialism [can be instituted at the state level]. And we have to send the right signals, from an electoral point of view. What do you want me to do, scare the bourgeoisie?"[23]

Though many of the bourgeois were indeed scared by the specter of an FA victory at the polls, upon taking office, the FA leaders shifted to the right, applying neoliberal policies and turning their backs on their leftist base in a cycle that has been all too common in the various left-of-center governments in the region. The victory of the FA is another example of grassroots momentum being channeled into what became a reformist electoral machine, and the reduction of a radical movement into a "lesser of two evils" election paradigm.

History's Dividends

On March 1, 2005, the night Tabaré Vázquez was inaugurated president, a sea of people, flags, and drum brigades surged through the streets of Montevideo. Fireworks pounded the air and car horns shrieked. The city bubbled with a cathartic happiness. The intoxicating sense of a break with the past and the possibility of real change in the future pushed citizens out into the streets to celebrate.

My interviews with various participants in the victory rallies exhibited a sense of the explosion of hope and enthusiasm. In spite of any reservations people had about the president's plans for the country, an almost religious fervor filled the city. "Vázquez's victory is a powerful change for Uruguay," asserted Martin Bension, a history teacher in Montevideo. "Now the people will have more opportunities to participate in the government. Right from the foundation of the Frente Amplio, decades ago, there has been popular participation in it. The Frente makes people feel more connected, so more people become involved." The fact that Vázquez was elected as part of the FA was significant; for many voters, the election was more about the party, and justice following the dictatorship, than it was about the candidate, especially since Vazquez himself did not participate in the FA's historic struggle.

Bension and others saw the election results as a direct nod to the battle against the dictatorship, and even a broader push toward unity and change in Latin America. "A lot of people died and went to jail in the seventies to win what the Frente Amplio has today," Bension said. "Besides improvements in Uruguay, the nations of Latin America should unite—just as Venezuelan President Hugo Chávez is trying to do—in spite of our soccer rivalries!" Indeed, one of the major differences between candidate Vázquez and his main opponent was his stated interest in collaborating with other leftist presidents in the region; Vázquez re-established ties with Cuba after Batlle had severed them.

Bands played in the streets and people waved flags, pounded drums, and drank the liquor stores dry to celebrate the inauguration. When the parties were over, some of this enthusiasm flowed back into the base committees of the FA. Whether or not the party would deliver was another issue, but in the euphoria following the inauguration, hope carried the day.

Shortly after Vázquez took office, the mood at an FA base committee in Montevideo was upbeat. The setting was typical of other party offices around the city: a cluttered meeting room with books and political pamphlets stacked along tables, a picture of Che

Guevara painted on the wall, and campaign posters plastered everywhere. People filed into the room, joking, patting each other on the
back and passing around yerba maté, a strong herbal tea popular in
Uruguay and Argentina.

Eventually participants sat down and introduced themselves.
They were carpenters, school teachers, plumbers, students, electri-
cians, unemployed people, and musicians. Some had been members
of the party for decades, and others were showing up for the first
time. They planned a cultural event with artists and musicians from
Uruguay and Cuba. Then, after lengthy discussions, they elected a
secretary, representative, and treasurer. Security in the neighborhood and the condition of one of the main roads was the next topic
of discussion.

Toward the end of the meeting, a long-standing member of the
base committee spoke to the group, making a pitch to new members:
"For those who just arrived for the first time, we ask for your participation. It doesn't matter if you don't know anything about politics.
You'll learn while you're here. With this new government in office,
the responsibility of the people is greater than ever before." Yet, in
the months following the election, regardless how much people at
that base committee and others participated, the party hierarchy
went in its own direction, pushing some of the same policies that had
created the 2002 economic crisis.

"A wild cat that has turned into a vegetarian"

At a dinner with businessmen at the Inter-American Development
Bank shortly after the election, Vázquez announced that Danilo
Astori would be the Minister of Economy and Finances for his government. The selection of Astori—a former leftist, but at that point a
proponent of neoliberalism—produced applause from the right and
condemnation from the left. Astori said he would carry on with the
economic policies of his predecessors, meaning a continued push for
the privatization of public services.

Once in the presidential palace, the FA administration decided
to pay off the country's external debt two years in advance, despite
progressive campaign promises to refuse to prioritize the payments.[24]

However, Vázquez did begin a "Social Emergency Plan" which allocated $100 million to social programs and relief for economic problems in areas such as housing, food, healthcare, and jobs.[25] Under Vázquez, poverty dropped from its 32 percent level in 2004, to 20 percent. The administration applied Ceibal Plan, which gives a laptop with an internet connection to every primary school student in the country,[26] and raised taxes for wealthy citizens.[27]

Given his election on a platform of change following the economic crisis, Vázquez was encouraged by his base to move away from a neoliberal economic model and provide expanded routes for popular participation in government. Instead, the president went a more reformist route, sprinkling his own neoliberal projects with social programs that didn't ultimately address the root causes of poverty and exclusion. And yet, given the record of past governments, these small nods to social change were enough to placate many voters.

Two years into the Vázquez administration's tenure, Argentina-based writer Marie Trigona wrote of the situation in Uruguay, "social movements have become stagnated with the crucial question of 'what next?'"[28] With the "lesser of two evils" in the presidential office, movements tend to demobilize, careful to offer tacit support rather than outright opposition. When the logic of electoral politics takes precedence over the urgent demands of a population, the role of social movements as powerful political protagonists can be lost or confused.

This is especially true when movements are drawn away from their demands and projects in order to participate in presidential campaigns. Leading up to the 2009 elections, in which former guerrilla leader and Agricultural Minister José Mujica was the FA candidate, the party's voter base helped ensure a victory for the party, as did the historic popularity of Vázquez, who enjoyed a 61 percent approval rating in October 2009.[29] This energy and momentum helped push Mujica into the presidency.

Upon taking office, Mujica appointed two other former imprisoned guerrillas to his government: Luis Rosadilla as the Minister of Defense and Eduardo Bonomi as the Minister of the Interior.[30] Danilo Astori, the former neoliberal Minister of Economy under Vázquez, became the vice-president. This combination of change and continuity is typical of the FA at this stage in its history, and highlights Galeano's warning of "celebration and comprise" at Mujica's inauguration.

Manuela Nieves, a housewife attending the inauguration with her daughter, said, "because of the all the years of suffering, we now deserve that the left remain in the government. Mujica represents the people. He will continue on the path of [former president] Tabaré but with a different heart."[31] The symbolic and cultural importance of the election of a former Tupamaro guerilla shouldn't be overlooked. But even Mujica himself admits to having given up part of his youthful idealism. As he said in the days leading up to the election, "we are not waiting for paradise, above all among the older people, but trying to escape from hell and cultivate hope."[32]

Hope buoyed and energized the FA for many years, paving its way into the presidential office for two consecutive terms following years of repression and persecution. The party members' survival instincts may be what led Mujica to "embrace serpents," as he put it, making compromises in order to get things done in politics.[33] The new president pledged to rid the country of extreme poverty and focus on Uruguay's neglected rural areas. At the same time, Mujica emphasized his desire to strengthen the private sector, increase wealth, and attract investment. For all of the new president's charisma, populist persona, and leftist background, his presidency is again likely to be characterized by moderation. In a gathering of businesspeople from Uruguay and Argentina, Mujica emphasized his personal political reformation, describing himself as a "wild cat that has turned into a vegetarian."[34]

As Uruguayan political science professor Juan Andrés Moraes explains, "Mujica says his government will be more like Brazilian President Lula's than the administrations of Evo Morales or Venezuela's Hugo Chávez. Basically, Mujica himself sees the differences clearly."[35] The presidents of these various countries are certainly different, as are the social movements that surround and pressure them. Over time, perhaps more radical ideas for fundamental change will percolate up from the base committees to the president, and the president will act on them. Or perhaps those same committees will be limited by their activities within the party. The FA's success as a political force in Uruguay may have led to electoral victories, but it also may have undermined some of the self-determination among its members.

Several FA members have realized and acknowledged this demobilizing dynamic within their movement. Helios Sarthou, a former FA senator and veteran lawyer for the FA, told journalist Michael Fox, "The issue of power is extremely serious. Companions of mine, that were together in the struggle... are today, all silent, exercising their positions in the conquest of power." Sarthou noted that the FA has shifted from its initial grassroots strategies to one of electoral advocacy. The left, he says, has in effect "converted its activists into voters."[36]

The creation of the communal council structure, among other initiatives and movements, however, leaves in Uruguay a cultural understanding of community participation in politics and social issues. Given a dire situation, the framework exists for grassroots organization and action. Such popular infrastructures, whether created by the state or a political party, can reap undeniable benefits; they can also constrain the autonomy of communities.

While the history and ongoing developments of the FA in Uruguay provides an interesting case study of the fusion of grassroots and political party activity, Venezuela provides even further insight into this dynamic. Under the presidency of Hugo Chávez, state- and party-created social programs and community projects have blurred the lines between the government and social movements in complex ways. The next chapter deals with the dance in Venezuela between a leftist government and a mobilized population, a relationship that is unique in both its harmony and dissonance.

Members of the Ezequiel Zamora National Campesino Front march in support of President Hugo Chávez's 2006 re-election bid, while also advocating for their own rights and autonomy. Photo by: Sílvia Leindecker

CHAPTER FIVE
Venezuela: Uses of the Bolivarian Revolution

The sounds of car horns, salsa music, children in playgrounds, barking dogs, and occasional gun shots rise out of Catia, one of the largest slums in South America. Catia is a sea of multi-tiered, tin-roofed brick shacks that cling to the mountains around Caracas, Venezuela. Uncollected garbage rots in the streets and tangled wires pirating electricity weave from house to house. Sporadically rising out of this neighborhood are dilapidated concrete apartment buildings with laundry flapping from the balconies like flags.

Much of the support for President Hugo Chávez, who was elected in 1998, comes from neighborhoods like Catia. Since taking office, Chávez has used his mandate as a leader, and the nation's oil wealth, to create programs that provide free education, dental and health clinics, land and housing reform, government-subsidized supermarkets, and hundreds of thousands of business cooperatives. In Venezuela, where much of the population lives below the poverty line, these programs have had an enormous impact.

Though Chávez and his party are popular, and continue to be re-elected and supported through ballot-box initiatives, there are causes for concern regarding the centralization of power under Chávez, and the creation and cooptation of social movements as part of the leader's electoral machine. Though these issues, present in Venezuela as well as other countries with left-leaning governments, are troubling, there is undeniable enthusiasm in Venezuela for Chávez's leadership and the changes his government has enacted. Furthermore, a number of government initiatives and policies have empowered the grassroots in unprecedented ways, and created space in which social movements can flex their muscles. Without the support of these movements, Chávez would not still be in power. And without Chávez's leadership, many of these movements would still be facing the type of repression they saw under previous administrations.

This dance between support and autonomy is complicated by the right wing, which poses a constant threat to both the advances of the Chávez administration and the movements. The right-wing opposition in Venezuela is powerful, with massive ties to the media and commercial sectors in the country. They have waged an all-out war on Chávez, his policies, his supporters, and the Venezuelan left in general. From the lies transmitted by their media monopolies to violent street protests and destabilization efforts, the Venezuelan right is a potent enemy for Chávez and the left, requiring sufficient responses in economic, political, and social arenas. The power of the right also complicates criticism of the Chávez administration from a leftist perspective.

Activism beyond the electoral realm that does not directly contribute to Chávez's power is widespread in Venezuela, and though it often goes unseen by media outside the country, it forms the backbone of the widely heralded social changes going on throughout Venezuela. Yet contradictions and challenges mix with enthusiasm, hope, and victories in the dance between the state and social movements in Venezuela.

Popular media organizations demonstrate one aspect of the political and social reality of Venezuela. Radio Rebelde set up shop in Catia in 2002 in a collection of buildings which are home to a small hospital, a cafeteria, and a giant garage turned into a refugee camp for hundreds of families whose homes were destroyed in one of the many mudslides that demolish entire Caracas hillside communities each year. When I visited the radio station in 2005, a group of men and women were sitting around drinking coffee and talking about an upcoming radio show. Among them was Jesús Arteaga, the unsalaried general coordinator of Radio Rebelde, who earns his living by cooking in El Comedor Libre, a free, government-funded community cafeteria.

"When Radio Rebelde started," Arteaga explained, "an assembly was held with members of the community to develop a way for the neighborhood to participate." Years later, the program schedule includes shows on local history, child care, natural medicine, ecology, and politics. There is a particular emphasis on promoting Venezuelan music and culture, to counter what Arteaga believes is the corporate media's objective of erasing local memory and traditions. "They want us to become global consumers. They want us to know who Britney Spears is, but not know that our own neighbor is a singer, not to know our own local values and histories."[1]

This initiative reflects a larger enthusiasm that characterizes the Bolivarian Revolution—the name used to the described the Chávez-led political movement pushing for the changes in the country. Radio Rebelde is one of many programs, radio stations, and projects started by community members, with support from the government, that have had a positive effect on the community. "The radio station isn't an end; it is a means to create community, a way to create a social network," said Arteaga. "People always stop by to drink a cup of coffee, converse—it's a social group." The radio is open to the community; regular classes and meetings are held to teach newcomers how to start their own programs. The station itself is run collectively by community members. According to Arteaga,

> When a big decision needs to be made regarding how the radio station works, there is an assembly that all of the program producers come to, and everyone has an equal say. We want all decisions to be made through consensus. If we vote, it is because we can't decide any other way.

Radio Rebelde demonstrates grassroots and government power coming together with a positive effect on the community. The station wouldn't have been able to start or continue broadcasting without government support, which makes up about 25 percent of its funding.

A visit to La Vega, another Caracas neighborhood, offered a close look into the grassroots activity in Venezuela—and also some of its challenges. La Vega, a sea of tin-roofed shacks and steep narrow streets, is one of the poorest neighborhoods in Caracas.

Calle y Media is a media collective located on a hilltop in La Vega. Katrina Kozarek, a member of the collective, introduced me to her friends in the neighborhood and pointed out the local Mercal, a common sight throughout Caracas. "Government subsidized food is sold here," she said. "At the Mercals everything is always cheaper. Here you can usually get the basic stuff." Next to the Mercal a building was under construction which was scheduled to include eight to twelve computers and offer free workshops on programming and the internet.[2] A block from Katrina's apartment was a two-story, octagonal building, home to the local Barrio Adentro health clinic. Katrina explained that service was swift at the clinic, and health services from medicine to checkups were free. Clinics of this kind had become widespread throughout the neighborhood. These projects, funded and organized by the government with the participation of the local community, have an undeniably positive impact on the daily lives of people living in La Vega.

Many poor Venezuelans see Chávez as a very different leader than those of the past. As one grandmother living in a poor neighborhood pointed out, "Chávez is the first president who even knows we are here. Our houses are still tin and cardboard, but now my grandchildren receive two meals a day in school. When times get really tough there is a Bolivarian Cafeteria up the hill, and there are several doctors living within walking distance who will see us and give us medicine for free."[3] These services make the daily lives of many Venezuelans less dire, and allow them opportunities to improve their standard of living.

Nearby the health clinic, a family spoke of their culture of activism, which is both critical and supportive of the Chávez government. The mother of the house, Alicia Cortez, also the Coordinator of the local Health Committee, explained how the *Comedores Libres*, or Free Cafeterias, worked. She had been running a government-funded cafeteria from her home for a year. Her husband, "Gordo" Edgar Lopez, was working at the Central University of Venezuela. Gordo, a jovial man with a huge smile, is also well-known drummer in the neighborhood.[4]

"We've been doing community work for decades," he explained, sitting down at a table in the kitchen. He believed that the participation of citizens in community activism has expanded and been better organized since Chávez came into office:

> People have been given more responsibility over their own lives. We support and defend the Chávez government, but we are very critical when we need to be. If there are no criticisms, the revolution dies. Socialism fails when people stop having a voice in the government. I don't believe in saviors, I believe in the people.

Gordo's sentiments were shared by dozens of people I spoke with in Venezuela. They represented enthusiasm and a will to make the most of Venezuela's current political situation, and work against the tendency of political momentum to get bogged down in bureaucracy and centralization. The community's acknowledgement of their part in initiating and perpetuating social change gives their movements more power and longevity than if they simply trusted the state to create and sustain the social programs in the barrios. As Marcelo of Calle y Media put it, "Chávez isn't the revolution, he's a part of it."

Another story, from the neighborhood of El 23 de Enero in Caracas is emblematic of the progressive changes taking place in the country. The 23 de Enero neighborhood has a history of social consciousness and rebellion. Many residents first arrive from rural areas, and slowly build their own brick houses into the hillside. As a poor neighborhood, El 23 de Enero was marked by police as a dangerous area, whose residents should be controlled. During conservative regimes, the local police station was a place of torture and imprisonment for many community leaders. After decades of state violence, the community has been able to reclaim and transform this center of repression. Juan Contreras, a radio producer, leader in the community organization Coordinador Simón Bolívar, and long-time resident of the neighborhood, talked about how he and his *compañeros* took over the police station—for decades an outpost for crackdowns on leftist organizing—and transformed it into a community radio station and cultural center.

"This place was a symbol of repression," Contreras explained to me in the studio, which still smelled like fresh paint from the recent conversion. "So we took that symbol and made it into a new one." He continued: "It is evidence of the revolution made by us, the citizens. We can't hang around waiting for the revolution to be made for us; we have to make the changes." The station receives state funding, but community members fought hard for permission to reclaim the police station by occupying the building without permission. El 23 de Enero's victories are examples of how Venezuelan movements have worked with the Chávez administration by demanding attention through direct action, and then working with state support after proving their dedication and community participation.[5]

Movements in Venezuela negotiate the same difficult space as other countries with potentially progressive administrations: how to wrest rights from the government without giving ammunition or attention to the right-wing opponents of the government. Iraida Morocoima is a part of the 5 de Julio Pioneer Camp Urban Land Committees, which fight for the titles to the land and homes where members already live. Their struggle is against both the opposition and the government bureaucracy. "[I]t's more difficult, because by opposing the government you may be helping the opposition and those same business interests. But fortunately, the people have been waking up, and they are more conscious. As a lot of us say, 'I am with Chávez. I am with Chávez as a tool. The guy is giving us a tool and we have to construct socialism [ourselves].'"[6]

The tactic, employed by many Venezuelan activists, of seizing upon the opportunities provided by the Chávez government, while also maintaining grassroots autonomy and momentum from below, is the foundation of many of the hopeful social changes going on in Venezuela today. This dynamic has less to do with Chávez's state programs and negotiations with social movements, though, and is more directly a result of Venezuela's political history, and the roots of Chávez and his political party.

Organizing Fury

Two decades ago, police and the military flooded the poor neighborhoods of Caracas, including Catia, La Vega, and El 23 de Enero. The city had risen up and taken to the streets in a revolt against President Carlos Andrés Pérez that eventually helped pave the way to the election of Chávez, and the state was striking back. When Pérez became president 1988, he appointed right-wing economists in his government and followed the IMF and World Bank's mandates for the Venezuelan economy, which included cutting subsidies to the poor, slashing welfare programs, and increasing fuel prices by 100 percent and transportation prices by 30 percent. On February 27, 1989, students led the initial protests against these measures by occupying the Caracas bus station and blocking roads. During this uprising, which came to be called the *Caracazo*, activists set up barricades on several roads and set a bus on fire. Community protests spread like wildfire across the city and country.[7]

One graffitied slogan written during the uprising was, "El pueblo tiene hambre" (The people are hungry). This hunger led people to take food from stores. However, in the light of the recent cost of living increases caused by Pérez's policies, poor Venezuelans saw their appropriation of food as a conscious act of civil disobedience. According to one report, "When people went into shops to take goods, they were often heard singing the national anthem as they did so, many carried the national flag and in many cases people organized the stealing of goods by lining up in an orderly manner." This organized fury was met with a new wave of state violence. Pérez responded by declaring martial law on February 28, sending in troops and police for massive repression.[8]

Blood filled the streets. In some cases security forces attacked poor neighborhoods long after the protests had ceased. Figures of citizens murdered in this campaign of state violence are between three hundred and three thousand.[9] During the conflict, Chávez was a young soldier in the Miraflores presidential palace, but was sick at the time, so didn't take part in the military repression. Within the ranks of the military, dissent had been growing against the Pérez administration for some time. When the president ordered soldiers to repress their own people, it was a breaking point. Chávez said that after the Caracazo he realized "that we had passed the point of no return and we decided that it was time to take up arms. We could not continue to be the custodians of a genocidal regime." Along with other officers and leftists, he began planning a coup against Pérez. At midnight on February 4, 1992, Chávez and six thousand troops made their move in Caracas and in six other Venezuelan cities. Tanks, paratroopers, and soldiers marched down the streets, displaying the power of their movement, and eventually arriving to attack Pérez in the Miraflores presidential palace. While this was a historic demonstration of populist sentiment and military force, it wasn't enough to overthrow the government.[10]

When Chávez realized that the uprising had failed, he surrendered on the condition that he be allowed to address the country in a televised address. The address lasted one minute, and in it he asked his fellow soldiers to lay down their weapons. Greg Wilpert, sociologist and founding editor of the online media outlet Venezuela Analysis, writes

> [Chávez's televised speech] gave a face to a military rebellion that enjoyed widespread popular support, turned him into a folk hero, both for taking responsibility for the failed rebellion—something practically no previous politician had ever done—and for suggesting that he would try again sometime because he said his group's objectives had not been achieved "for now."[11]

The coup, and the subsequent surrender, made Chávez into a national figure representing the left and opposition to the Peréz regime.

Following his surrender, Chávez then spent two years in prison. When Rafael Caldera became president in 1994, he followed through on his campaign promise to release Chávez from jail and offer amnesty to him and others who had been active in the coup. Chávez then began to build a political party. With his eyes on the 1998 election, he formed the Movement for the Fifth Republic (MVR), a name that suggested a new Republic of Venezuela, following four past refoundations of the country over its history.[12] The MVR didn't emerge directly out of a social movement, as was the case with the Workers' Party in Brazil, the MAS party in Bolivia, and even the candidacy of Kirchner in Argentina. Instead, it arose as a vehicle to propel Chávez into power and only later developed strong ties with social movements. From the beginning, the party and Chávez himself, as a military officer, enjoyed significant support from the military.[13]

In 1998, Chávez began a presidential campaign that took him across the country, soliciting support from diverse sectors of society. He started out with little financial backing, often traveling in a broken-down pickup truck and giving speeches out of the back. His humble background—he grew up in a poor family—and fiery speeches offered a radical alternative to the wealthy, right-wing politicians in power and gave hope to a disenfranchised population. He won the 1998 election with 56.2 percent of the vote.

After taking office, Chávez made good on his promise to "refound the republic" and convened a constituent assembly to rewrite the constitution. The subsequent document became a fundamental part of the "Bolivarian Revolution," a collection of programs and political processes initiated by the Chávez administration, and named after Venezuela's nineteenth-century liberator, Simón Bolívar. In 1999, in a move spearheaded by Chávez, the constitution was completely overhauled through a series of referendums and editing sessions that took place in government offices and neighborhood assemblies across the country.

One major shift created by the new constitution was that the state was granted full ownership of the Petroleos de Venezuela SA (PDVSA) gas and oil company. PDVSA had been a state-run oil company since the 1970s, though was not officially recognized as such by the previous constitution.[14] This regulation keeps the government, instead of corporations, in control of the industry. The law states that all government activity connected to oil production and exploration is to be devoted to the "public interest," and toward supporting "the organic, integrated, and sustainable development of the country."[15]

The largest oil and gas reserves in Latin America are found in Venezuelan subsoil. For decades, a small elite profited from the industry while the majority of citizens lived in poverty. With Chávez's rise to power, this vicious cycle began to change. Through a renegotiation of contracts with foreign petroleum industries, Chávez officially transferred much of Venezuela's oil into state hands. Once the new contracts were in place, the revenue from the business was redirected away from the country's elite and largely spent on programs in health care, literacy, education, and subsidized food for poor communities.[16] Additionally, a change in the tax system was designed to generate more income for the government. The reform established an unprecedented rise in taxes from 16.6 percent to 30 percent per barrel in 2001, followed by increases of up to 50 percent per barrel of oil in later years, with payments directed to the government.

However, the elites didn't take kindly to these changes. A two month long oil strike in 2002–2003 led by right-wing business and union leaders sought to destabilize the country and overthrow

Chávez. The strike, which took place within PDVSA, cost the Venezuelan economy an estimated $20 billion. After the devastating strike ended, Chávez replaced twelve thousand workers, and "renationalized" this company. In this way, the strike helped pave the way to an expansion of the Chávez administration's power over the industry, and subsequently increased state regulation and funds to the government.[17]

Bolivarian Tools and Spaces

Leading up to his election and during his initial time in office, people came to believe in Chávez as a powerful figure who represented their interests. His popularity was based in part on a public perception of him as an advocate of the poor. This reputation buoyed support and was strengthened by the diverse social programs the Chávez administration created in the country. Though important contradictions and challenges have emerged throughout his time in power, the support for his leadership should not be underestimated.

Peggy Ortiz is a blonde, self-proclaimed *Chávista* (Chávez supporter) in Caracas. "People believe in Chávez. I believe in him," Ortiz explained as we walked in downtown Caracas. "He's a clean president. He doesn't hide anything. Most people who are against Chávez don't understand this political process."[18] Many of the neoliberal presidents who preceded Chávez were far from representing the people in any way, and primarily repressive and exploitative. Rather than needing to operate clandestinely as in the past, many leftist groups and movements can now operate in the open, with support from the government. In this sense, Chávez is progressive and popular compared to his predecessors.

William Barillas, a tall, bearded volunteer at Radio Horizante, a community radio station in Merida, a mountainous state in western Venezuela, shared Ortiz's enthusiasm for the president. He believes that the Chávez administration is a significant improvement from previous governments. "This government has left the era when governments never did anything for the country. They used to just help capitalists, which were a minority of the population. This government actually cares about the education and health of poor people."[19] This opinion was common among the dozens of people I spoke with during a 2005 visit to Venezuela: that Chávez was wonderful compared to the past. However, endorsements for his policies and presidency, even those with a critical edge, spanned a wider array of opinions.

When Yolanda Zerpa, a coffee farmer in a mountainous region outside Merida, found her farmland and home destroyed by a mudslide, the government provided a low interest loan to help her get back on her feet. She explained that she wouldn't have been able to get a loan from a typical bank due to her dire economic situation. The government's help was crucial, even though she admitted she is not a devout follower of Chávez. "I have never been interested in politics," she explained. "It divides people and communities. I just do what work I can to support my family."[20] Some Venezuelans, like Zerpa, appreciate the government simply because of the added resources it offers that make everyday struggles in the country easier to bear. This was echoed by Jesus Gavidia, a telephone worker I spoke with during his lunch break in a wealthy Caracas neighborhood. "The poor love Chávez because, with him, they see a way out of poverty."[21]

Many Chávez supporters are quick to point to the variety of programs initiated across the country thanks to the government's willingness and funds from the nationalized oil industry. These programs not only alleviate poverty and provide access to education and healthcare for a sector of society that has perhaps never received such services, but they empower people through the creation of neighborhood councils, cooperatives, and land committees. On this point, Venezuelan history professor Margarita López Maya speaks of the attraction to the Chávez government and its empowering effects.

> Almost all of his administration's social policies involve organization and participation. You say, "We need a Cuban doctor here," and the government will facilitate it once you organize a health committee. You say, "We want to own the property on which we built the house we have lived in for thirty years," and the government will give you ownership once you fulfill certain requirements, such as organizing an urban land committee through a citizen assembly. You have the right—and the encouragement—to do all that now.[22]

This support network created by the government with the participation of the people has been widely used. One example is Venezuela's Housewives' Union. A group of women formed the union based on an article in the new constitution which guarantees the welfare and health of housewives, and their right to an education and suitable home. The union began in 2003 and has grown to include over a hundred thousand women from across the country, many of whom have few economic resources and are widowed or single.[23]

Lizarde Prada, the General Coordinator of the Housewives' Union for the state of Merida, spoke with me in a cluttered office that is the center of the union's activities. The walls of the office were covered with portraits of President Chávez and anti-Iraq War posters. Prada was animated throughout the interview, clearly deeply involved in the union's work. Her two cell phones rang constantly and union workers rushed in and out of the office.

"We, the union, are a channel that is showing people a different direction. Often these women don't know that there is money, there are resources available. It's just a matter of knowing where they are," Prada said.[24] The union helps members understand the rights and resources they are entitled to as citizens and housewives. It provides legal support to their members and informs them of the free educational, medical, and subsidized food programs the government provides. Prada explained that the union offers classes on starting cooperatives for business and community work. "For example, if you live in a certain neighborhood and you have the raw materials, such as bananas, use it for a sweets shop and use local transportation for your business." Some of the cooperatives affiliated with the Housewives' Union include food production and distribution, others have to do with textiles and sewing.

The union grew out of the space—both real and psychological—created by the new constitution, and now operates in a symbiotic and independent relationship with the state, guiding women toward government subsidies and programs, but also empowering union members. "Many of our women are inside their homes all the time," Prada noted. "In the house they work as cooks, decorators, teachers, babysitters, and doctors—all of this in one person. Our union helps to empower the housewives. Many of them were stuck in their homes, they didn't have time to read or write, they were always cooking and cleaning, they weren't informed. Many of our women are opening their eyes now."

Dozens of government programs have encouraged such activism. For Venezuelans involved in community organizing and politics today, many have been empowered by the current government in ways they never experienced under previous administrations. The new constitution acts as an arm, or tool, for implementing government programs. Citizens are empowered by this new aspect of the constitution, but did they need the constitution to recognize these rights? The state, in this case, is seen as a fundamental legitimizing force within a system that enables programs and unions like this to emerge, but doesn't transform the basic social and economic structure the government operates in. Yet, this story underscores the importance of the relationship between the government and the people, and how progressive policies can empower certain sectors of the population.

Power and the People

Perhaps the most visible contradiction in the Bolivarian Revolution is the position of Chávez himself as the central figure. As with Morales in Bolivia, the entire structure of the party and political process is centered around his personality, power, and charisma. However popular he may be, the centralization of power inherent in the process begs the question: can the Bolivarian Revolution outlast Chávez? A number of experts on Venezuela have weighed in on this issue of centralized power, and the counterweight provided by social movements in the country.

Analyst Edgardo Lander explains that the general dependency on Chávez weakens the political process, and that the president's "style of leadership could become an obstacle to a process of democratization if many of the key decisions of the process remain in his hands, thereby closing the door to the urgent necessities of the institutionalization of public administration and of the organization and autonomy of the popular movement."[23] The danger of the revolution getting bogged down in such bureaucracy means that the process, as it is designed now, cannot flow smoothly without Chávez involved.

This need for Chávez as the leader poses a series of dilemmas. Former *NACLA Report on the Americas* editor Fred Rosen notes that many of the groups in the dynamic Venezuelan civil society, "are fiercely loyal to Chávez, rather than to any particular political party or program."[26] This cult of personality was certainly present during my visits to the country. Few conversations took place without mentioning Chávez as a key element of funding, projects, policies, and current events in general. "The process," Luis Serrano, a Chávista union leader explained, "begins with Chávez and his motivational power, and then builds mechanisms through which to exercise power. But many have no point of reference other than that their leader is Chávez."[27] If the popularity of the government is based solely on Chávez, that too has a weakening effect on the revolution; he won't live forever and he could always be voted out of office. More resilient, extra-electoral institutions and autonomous movements are essential for sustaining a long-term transformation of society.

But where would the movements in Venezuela be without Chávez? Many of them exist and are empowered to act because of his government. Once movements accept state funding, a structure of movement subordination to the state is created. When movements establish themselves, analyst James Petras points out, the reformist entities within the government seek to "convert the movements into transmission belts of state policy."[28] The work of many organizations and projects initiated by the state is confined to operating within the realm of party politics and the logic of the state, which by its nature seeks a concentration, rather than diffusion, of power. In the end, will the need to "defend" Chávez fall away, as the needs of the community take center stage? That will be *Chávismo*'s ultimate test: if the changes can proceed without Chávez.

In the meantime, many people are benefiting from government programs and projects. Yet, creating social movements and grassroots organization "from above" also creates a series of challenges. As political science professor Sara Motta illustrates in an assessment of social programs in La Vega, while access to healthcare certainly helps people's lives, the institutionalization of social movements in this process can be harmful to community organizing. "[H]ealth can become a particular issue solved in a functional manner that undermines the community's organization and therefore the development of a participatory social democracy. Individuals who were once organizers of their communities become functionaries of the state." Motta explains this can have a weakening effect on the community's autonomy and capacity to self-organize.[29]

Similar issues arise with other government-sponsored programs, such as *Misión Ribas*, a nationwide educational program that organizes classes in neighborhoods to meet local needs. Students use their education to solve immediate problems with projects and planning. Elizabeth, a participant in this process who has organized classes across La Vega, largely with women, said, "It has been an emancipatory experience for me and many others who have begun to believe in their ability to solve problems in the community."[30] Yet, in seeking to address a public service problem, writes Motta, the education "seeks to enable the student to find solutions for particular problems, such as inadequate housing, within the limits of broader structures of power. In doing so it attempts to democratize these broader structures, but not transform them."[31] The broad-based government programs can have liberating effects, but only within the confines of the existing state structure.

Greg Wilpert says that some of these expanded democratic practices are undermined by the government's continued focus on the president as the central source of decision-making: Chávez can personally choose ministers and begin new ministries, declare states of emergency, and so on. In general, the government is very centralized around Chávez and the clientelism inherent in such a system. Wilpert writes, "The result is that it is difficult for Venezuela's civil society and social movements to find a voice that is independent of that of the president, without automatically becoming branded as being part of the opposition."[32]

As an extension of this clientelism, the *boliburgesia* (a word made up of *boli* for Bolivarian, and *burgesia* for bourgeois) has formed as a class of people who have profited from the Bolivarian Revolution, and see it as no more than a way to earn money and gain employment. Such a byproduct is nothing new; people have been seeking opportunities from governments in Venezuela throughout the country's history. The difference this time, however, is the extent to which the government says it is working for the people, and then proceeds to empower a new class of elites.[33]

There are both reformist and more radical currents among government officials and politicians within the Bolivarian Revolution that continue to play tug-of-war over the direction of the country. Some want a more participatory civil society, while others see social programs and supportive movements simply as conduits of state power to be called upon for votes and momentum in electoral campaigns; turning activists into voters, as with the Frente Amplio party in Uruguay.

The typical problems associated with governments across the hemisphere persist in Venezuela, in spite of gains in the social programs' ability to alleviate poverty in the short term. Though they have improved the lives of many impoverished Venezuelans, the missions have encountered bureaucratic setbacks: sometimes citizen stipends are delayed, or seeds germinate en route to agricultural cooperatives.[34] A similar challenge is posed by the government's reliance on oil money—funding that is as much in flux as the price of oil, and due to disappear when the oil does, leaving social programs at the mercy of the oil market.

Besides remaining inserted into the labyrinth of global capitalism, the Bolivarian state, however benevolent in the eyes of the people, still replicates the inequalities and challenges found in many other nations. These realities have a profound impact on the functionality of the Bolivarian Revolution itself.

Beyond Governance

Communal councils offer an interesting look into some of the participatory aspects of the Bolivarian process. They were created by the government in 2006, and thousands of them exist across the country today. The councils work to solicit funding from the government, begin social projects, programs, and missions in their community, and deal with issues like the management of local health and water projects.[35]

Long-time Venezuelan activist Alfonso Olivo believed the

communal councils were "the most revolutionary measure that this government has taken" due to their transfer of power from mayors and governors to the ordinary citizens in the councils. "The people are capable [of social planning] by themselves, without the involvement of the state or the bureaucratic officials," he noted.[36]

Communal councils in Venezuela show the fascinating push and pull that emerges where the state creates structures and projects that build community bonds. The councils are sometimes autonomous from, or even antagonistic toward, the Bolivarian state and party. It is essential to contextualize the political landscape of this grassroots space before dissecting some of the dynamics of the dance.

The Chavez administration organized the councils in ways that encourage community involvement. Anyone over the age of fifteen can participate, and for a decision to be officially made, at least 30 percent of those in the council have to vote on it. In urban areas, councils must involve a minimum of 150 families, and around 20 families in rural areas.[37] This scale means that the councils promote direct participation and are relatively easy to self-manage. When a council comes to a decision for a project, they can receive funding directly from the national government or national institutions, dispersing power away from local mayors and officials and into the hands of residents themselves.[38] Communal councils have provided a check to the power of local governments, as well as a platform to demand transparency and a more efficient bureaucracy from the government.

The smaller scale and local focus of these councils is essential to their sustainability. As political scientist Josh Lerner points out, "Since the councils usually contain only a couple hundred families within a few blocks, their members tend to be socio-economically, demographically, and politically similar. Since residents decide the boundaries of their own councils, they can self-select like-minded groups." This means that they can pinpoint community needs and decide on projects more efficiently than a state official who doesn't live in the neighborhood. Lerner gives the following example: "If the members of the 23 de Enero council obviously need a new elevator, because of their common situation and interests, it may be in their best interest to pursue the elevator without spending much time and energy debating it."[39] Localized control is at the heart of the council's functionality, helping to eliminate unnecessary bureaucracy and circumvent corrupt or unresponsive politicians.

The councils can also provide a counterweight to a more centralized state. Sara Motta writes that the communal councils "are an attempt to create a new set of state institutions that bypass the traditional state, and distribute power in a democratic and participatory manner."[40] The elasticity of the relationship between the grassroots and the state is tested here through a public empowered by state-created institutions—institutions that citizens can then use to challenge the traditional state if necessary.

The balancing act between remaining autonomous from the state and engaging it is described by council participant Edenis Guilarte, "We must obtain the tools to be able to struggle against the bureaucracy and search for a way to get rid of leaders who want to control us, look to maintain their own power, and who divide the community." In this sense, the councils can be a tool of emancipation. "What we are doing," Guilarte explained, "is training, creating consciousness, which is a process that goes beyond repairing a road, obtaining a service, enabling access to water. It's a macro process, a process of social change, a fight over ideas and practice."[41] The social bonds created by working on development projects through these state-created institutions can supersede the immediate goals of the actual project.

While communal councils manage budgets and develop community projects, they also serve as a basis for networking and developing community ties, which are then useful beyond the councils' work. For example, Ismila, a community activist in a Caracas neighborhood, explained that when the public water company Hidrolara didn't respond to demands from her community to deal with a sewage backup for two days, the members of her communal council decided to take matters into their own hands. Because they were used to working together, debating and organizing, it was easy to coordinate a trip to the Hidrolara offices and demand to speak with the person in charge of dealing with sewage emergencies. Together, they had to pressure the officials for two hours, but ended up returning to their community with an engineer to take care of the problem. Ismila said, "We learned today that Hidrolara is useless as an institution, it does not work for the communities. These officials think they know everything and don't listen to the community until there's a problem."[42] So while the bureaucracy posed a problem, the solidarity and sense of community developed through the communal councils helped to solve it.

The central question of the political struggle within this space, according to Motta, is whether the communal councils will "become an institution that channels the demands of poor communities to a localized social democracy (with all the possibilities and limitations that this entails) or whether they enable the expansion of demands for community self-management that challenge capitalist social relations."[43] The councils provide the tools for local organizing, which has a great potential to dismiss government clientelism and assert autonomy, helping people to live and organize beyond the state.

There are a number of cases in which social movements and groups—both created autonomously and by the government—have risen up, either in defiance of the Chávez government or with positions that radicalize the government's policies. Some have been organized around environmental, labor, and political issues and deserve attention here. As the editors of the book *Venezuela Speaks!* point out, the Bolivarian Revolution depends on grassroots activism. The future of the revolution, they write, "does not just depend on whether it can continue to overcome the destabilization and fear campaigns of the opposition. It also depends on how well the government is able to listen to the voices demanding even deeper changes."[44] The government's response to criticism and protest from the left gives a very clear message of how much power and space it is willing to cede.

Blurring the Lines

The collaboration between movements and the state can result in a certain blurring of the lines between the two entities. Such confusion benefits the government to the extent that it can utilize movements for electoral and political ends. Social movements and grassroots organizations in the country have been able to defend their autonomy and interests more effectively when they remain aware of the very real gap between their own power and that of the state, and when they don't allow themselves to be absorbed into the state institutionally or ideologically.

The lines between the movements and the state can become particularly blurred during electoral campaigns and referendums. Aspects of the electoral and political fight from below to defend Chávez have strengthened social bonds in the country, tightening the fabric of community life, while empowering the government.

Movement for the Fifth Republic "Party Electoral Battle Units" and "Electoral Patrols" were government initiatives utilized by Venezuelan citizens in the lead-up to the August 15, 2004 referendum on whether or not to have a recall vote on the Chávez presidency. Journalist Jonah Gindin wrote, "Every Venezuelan who did not want to see Chávez removed from office was encouraged to organize him or herself into a 'patrol' of ten committed activists." Over one million joined the campaign almost immediately. Some of those who joined were experienced activists and organizers, but many were becoming involved in political activism for the very first time—a clear showing of the complex and vital collaboration between the bases and the party.[45] The referendum on the recall vote was successful for Chávez supporters: 58 percent of voters were against the recall vote, in a strong showing that reinvigorated the president's mandate.[46]

The momentum following the 2004 referendum benefited Chávez in the 2006 presidential election, when he was re-elected with over 60 percent of the vote. His main rival was right-wing figurehead and Zulia state governor Manuel Rosales.[47] Following this re-election, political party leaders formed the United Socialist Party of Venezuela (PSUV) in March of 2007, to unite various left-wing parties in Venezuela—including Chávez's Movement for the Fifth Republic (MVR)—under one Bolivarian umbrella. The party was organized to be participatory, with leaders elected at local, regional, and national committee levels. The MVR Electoral Battle Units and Electoral Patrols were brought into the big PSUV tent as well. The party has grown to include seven million members, playing a central role in contemporary Venezuelan electoral politics.[48]

In the wake of these victories, a December 2007 referendum on further changes to the constitution backfired for Chávez. Fifty-one percent of voters shot down the 69 proposed amendments which included allowing for more state control over the economy and banking system, permitting Chávez to remain in office for consecutive terms (pending re-election), an extension of presidential terms from six to seven years, cutting the work day from eight to six hours, lowering the voting age from eighteen to sixteen, and expanding social security coverage to workers in the informal sector.[49] The proposed reforms only won 4.5 million votes, though the PSUV boasted 5 million members at the time.[50] Abstention in the elections rose from a level of 25 percent in the 2006 presidential election to 45 percent in the 2007 referendum. Many of the abstainers were from the Chávista ranks, but they weren't defecting to the right, they just weren't voting.

There are a number of reasons for the referendum's failure and abstention, and many of them strike at the heart of the Chávez administration's collaboration with its base of voters and activists. Some voters disagreed with certain reforms, believing they could be taken care of through legislation rather than constitutional changes. Others were disenchanted with the fact that these new reforms were being pushed through without much discussion between the grassroots of the Bolivarian Revolution and the government; they were largely being applied from on high.[51]

Sociology professor and journalist Sujatha Fernandes explains that a point of contention among voters was the fact that the proposed reforms were "decided by a small group of representatives in the National Assembly, rather than being debated in a larger and more inclusive decision-making body such as the Constituent Assembly." She writes that various campesino, media, Afro-Venezuelan, urban, and occupied factory social movements supported the reforms, but were critical of the decision-making process that developed the proposed changes. A document from this coalition of movements states that the reforms were decided upon "between four walls and without giving space to the people as the primary constituent." This lack of discussion contributed to the abstention and opposition among voters who formerly supported other Chávez policies and ballot-box initiatives.[52]

Overall, however, Chávista electoral strategies have politicized, oriented, and initiated countless Venezuelans into the world of political activism. Such ties remain regardless of the occupant of the presidential palace, and might easily serve autonomous causes. Such has been the case among certain labor, farming, and indigenous groups.

Appropriating the Revolution From Below

The Chávez government has worked to open up spaces for community organizing, like that of communal councils and cooperatives, but also for mobilizing to defend the Bolivarian Revolution from the attacks of the right-wing opposition. One salient, widely discussed case was the popular movement against the short-lived, Washington-backed, right-wing coup against President Chávez in April 2002. Thanks to support for Chávez from citizen-activists and the military, the attempt lasted less than two days.[53] During this coup, the Venezuelan people mobilized autonomously and spontaneously. Their ability to spring to action was largely based on the social fabric of existing community organizing and their enthusiasm for the Bolivarian process in the country. When movements mobilize against the right in defense of Chávez and the political process, the movements' specific needs and goals can be undermined and pushed aside. However, they can also intersect with those of the government.

In 2005, the Chávez administration announced decrees that enabled the state to expropriate businesses and factories to allow workers to manage them as cooperatives.[54] With the legal steps in place for the state to intervene when a factory or business shuts its doors, the government can now collaborate with the workers to make sure the business continues and the workers remain employed. Furthermore, under worker self-management, workers have control over major decisions about how their workplace is organized. Dozens of businesses across Venezuela have come under state and worker control. This is a dynamic example of a state-movement relationship that allows for broader grassroots autonomy.[55]

In 2005, workers took control of Inveval, a valve-producing business on the outskirts of Caracas. Pablo Cormenzana of Inveval explained that the plant shut down on December 9, 2002, leaving the workers out of jobs. "Originally, there were 330 workers at the plant.

A group of these workers decided to begin a fight to demand that the former owner pay them back what he owed them. Later, this demand transformed into the idea of recovering their jobs and to re-open the company." This legal and political battle went on for two years. Cormenzana recounted:

> The group was really dispersed at that time and in December 2004 only one worker continued to camp outside the factory. Around this time, the former boss decided that it was the perfect moment to empty out the factory. Until December, groups of workers had been camping outside the plant's doors. One night, the boss secretly began to transport the semi-constructed valves and tools from the plant. The workers found out that the owner was stealing material from the plant and re-mobilized. This time, more workers camped outside the company's doors so that the boss wouldn't continue to ransack the plant. They were thinking "this guy left us out in the streets and now he's leaving with the few things that could be sold to pay us back what he owed us."[56]

Their company went under state control in April of the following year. "Not only are the workers at Inveval successfully running a company without bosses or an owner, they're also doing it without technocrats or bureaucracy from the government. The government has had little participation in the functioning of the company," Cormenzana explained in 2006. "All of the workers make the same salaries, it doesn't matter if they are truck drivers, line workers, or the president of the company. They are putting into practice genuine worker control at Inveval."[57] Operations at the factory have continued in this vein in spite of bureaucratic setbacks and market competition.[58] Inveval provides an interesting example of empowered workers taking charge to push the government to operate as a tool for the workers, rather than the other way around.

Like worker-run factories in Argentina, Inveval serves a variety of purposes for the community and the government. The factory provides space for government mission programs and communal council meetings. The workers often organize political forums and host students and workers from other occupied factories around the world. The Venezuelan state has played more of an active role in worker-management than its counterpart in Argentina: though the workers make most of the major decisions affecting the company in their own workers assemblies, 51 percent of the business is owned by the state, and 49 percent by the workers.[59] Other recuperated businesses in Venezuela include a variety of cooperatives, state-owned businesses, and joint ventures like Inveval.

Such direct-action tactics have also worked in the area of land distribution. Article 307 of the new constitution calls for the break-up of large, private land holdings. Often, this policy change would have remained only on paper and never been implemented if not for the initiative of landless Venezuelans. Direct action forced the government to respond. In the state of Cojedes, for example, the governor granted land titles to small farmers only after they had actually occupied land, which in this case was owned by a private company in England. The government, seeking a resolution to long-standing land conflicts elsewhere, began to break up some twenty-one estates in 2005 for distribution to small farmers.[60] A vibrant civil society demonstrated it was ready and willing to move outside of the bounds of the government, using the state's own rhetoric to push the Chávez administration to action.

While the changes in the constitution have empowered some sectors of society, the politicized movements in the country have also run into challenges with the ingrained privilege and impunity that is a byproduct of government bureaucracy. Though farmers have occupied much land, campesinos have also faced repression from thugs hired by landowners opposed to the new agrarian policies: over two hundred campesinos have been killed since 2009. So far, only one landowner has been punished for his actions, due in part to the slow bureaucratic pace of the justice system.[61]

A conflict related to Venezuela's coal mining industry is similarly illustrative. For years, many Bar, Yukpa, and Wayúu indigenous people from western Venezuela have demanded an end to the coal mining in their lands on the Sierra de Perijá mountain range. The indigenous people say the destructive mining operations pollute the environment and water supply, and spread illness among local inhabitants. The dust produced by the open-pit coal mines has generated respiratory problems among local inhabitants, another reason for the exodus of many indigenous communities over the past fifteen years.[62] Four hundred million tons of coal are estimated to exist in the Sierra de Perijá region, an amount that could be mined for another half century. Much of the coal mining is carried out by companies that are consortiums formed between private international companies and the Venezuelan state company, Corpozulia. The destructive mining operations go on with the collusion of the right-wing Zulia state government, which has power over the justice system and police force.[63]

In 2006, indigenous people marched in Caracas for a meeting with government officials, but were blocked from arriving by 150 riot police. They wanted to speak with Chávez to denounce the mining operations and demand more say in how their lands were used by extractive industries, a right guaranteed to them in the 1999 constitution. They protested as supporters of Chávez, but with criticisms about the government's policies on mining.[64] As Wayúu leader Jorge Montiel said,

> What good is all this wealth from oil and coal if we are dying of diseases and misery? Several years ago, they pushed out some of our people to make a coal mine. In that region the animals, the fish, the birds, and the people are all sick. Now they want us to move again so they can make more mines, but there is nowhere to go.[65]

Even looking at the industry from a national perspective, the government's cooperation doesn't make sense as a part of a program of state socialism. Lusbi Portillo, a professor at the University of Zulia and the director of Homo et Natura, an environmental NGO, explained, "Coal mining doesn't serve the interests of Venezuelans or Zulians. It serves the interests of coal mining multinationals already operating in the country."[66]

In spite of such criticisms, Corpozulia pushed for further coal exploration, and has extended its reach into the region's grassroots organizations. Journalist James Suggett wrote in 2008,

> The state company is asserting various forms of control over local
> community councils, promising to help indigenous communities
> become shareholders in the future coal projects, and hiring infil-
> trators of indigenous descent to carry out the company's media
> campaign and intelligence work with a lower profile.[67]

Though new coal mining concessions in the Sierra de Perijá
have been suspended, coal mining still continues in various major
mines. In this case, a reliance on extractive industries to fuel state
programs went up against the livelihood of the indigenous people—
much as is the case in Ecuador.

When empowered groups of citizens and movements have risen
up against the Chávez government, some have been repressed or
ignored, while others were welcomed to the negotiating table or
granted support. Throughout these various projects, conflicts, and
relationships, the Venezuelan public has demonstrated the time-
tested capacity to utilize the state as a people's tool, and collaborate
with it when the causes of the people and the government intersect.
The broad presence of the Chávez administration in grassroots
spaces has indeed presented complicated challenges to movements.
At the same time, the relationship between the two entities has often
been mutually beneficial. Can either of the two exist without the
other? That remains an ongoing test for the broad umbrella of the
Bolivarian Revolution.

Immediately to the south of Venezuela, in Brazil, another working class leader rose to the presidency on the shoulders of labor and
agrarian movements. President Lula, once applauded as an ally of
the left and hope for the region, has all but betrayed the movements
that paved his way to power. The story of his administration's relationship with the enormous Brazilian landless movement is the focus
of the next chapter.

Landless movement activists marching on their way to occupy land they won in Rio Grande do Sul, Brazil.
Photo by: Michael Fox

CHAPTER SIX

Brazil: Lula and the Landless

Hundreds of grassroots movements and organizations converged at the 2005 World Social Forum in Porto Alegre, Brazil. Sandal-clad activists slept in tents by the side of the river and attended an array of workshops connected to grassroots struggles. The hope and global synergy was palpable in the incense-filled air. However, for many Brazilians, the bitter scent of betrayal soured the gathering. The unpopularity of President Luiz Inácio Lula da Silva's (Lula) Workers' Party (PT) among leftists at the forum fueled a fire of discontent against Lula as a traitor of the movements.

Venezuelan president Hugo Chávez was scheduled to speak in a massive arena during one evening at the forum. The crowds swarmed, packing the stadium. Typically, Lula would have accompanied Chávez to the event; the Brazilian president was met with exuberant applause at the 2003 forum after his election. Now, however, members of his own party couldn't even walk onto the stage without being booed off. Indeed, before Chávez took to the microphone, and the massive crowd was still filing into their seats, a member of Lula's administration rose to speak only to be drowned out by boos and whistles. This animosity against the PT was widespread at the forum, and represented a more national sense of outrage at the president.

How had Lula, once so widely heralded and loved by the Brazilian and international left, come to be essentially booed off the stage at the left's biggest global gathering? This chapter discusses the social and civic momentum that brought Lula, a working-class Brazilian into the presidential palace with a mandate to address the vast inequalities of Brazilian wealth, land ownership, and urban landscapes, and Lula's ultimate betrayal of these movements.

When Lula was elected, progressives and liberals in the US believed the victory signaled new hope for the region. They celebrated his victory, but as Lula immediately veered down a neoliberal path, international criticisms were few and far between. What happened to Lula? Why did he shift to the right? How was he constrained? And how did the movements in Brazil react? These questions will be addressed here. But first, to grasp the trajectory of Lula, his party, and the grassroots reaction to his presidential politics, it is important to understand the history of the country's biggest and most successful social movement: the Landless Workers Movement (MST).[1]

Strength in Numbers

In the early hours of the morning on October 29, 1985, 2,500 landless families arrived in trucks, buses, and motorcycles to occupy Fazenda Annoni, a 9,500 hectare plot of land in Rio Grande do Sul, Brazil. The families were forced to occupy the land out of desperation: half of the land in Brazil is owned by just 2 percent of the population.[2] For many of these activists, the alternative was grueling, slave-like labor on large estates, or crushing poverty in city slums. Darci Bonato, a participant in the occupation, recalled that the families had only what they could carry on their backs with them to start their new lives.

> We had a [grill] that we could use over an open fire, saucepans, food and bedclothes. The children had fallen asleep by the time we arrived and we laid them on a mattress under a tree, covering them with a blanket. Then we went back to the road to help guard the camp. That first night, none of the adults slept. There was a full moon, I remember, and it was quite bright. When dawn came, some policemen arrived. Strung out along the fence, we were ready to stop them coming in. There were rumors that we were armed, but we weren't. The only weapons we had were our hoes and scythes.[3]

Police tried to in vain to push them off the land, but the activists had strength in numbers, and successfully resisted the police as they continued preparing for their new lives. "People began putting up their tents, collecting water from the river, and lighting a fire for the cooking," Bonato recalled.[4]

The police siege of the camp went on for a year, making it hard for the families to come and go, and receive food and supplies. The MST activists eventually opened up a school to teach their children, and more people joined family members in the camp as it became further established. The police blockade made it necessary for everyone in the camp to share supplies, labor, and food. At one point, children approached the police and gave them flowers, explaining that they weren't against the police, but against the government. By 1987, the government agreed to let the farmers stay on the land. Bonato spoke of the years she spent at the camp:

> I don't regret it. If hadn't done that, I would have worked for thirty years as a farm laborer and ended up without a single hectare. So for me it was a huge victory. Today my sons are living on the settlement with me, each with his plot of land. They lived through it all with me, and now they're ten times better off than they would have been if I'd gone on working as a hired hand.[5]

The MST members who occupied Fazenda Annoni saw the direct rewards of their hard work, and inspired new landless activists in Brazil.

The tactics of the MST speak to the creativity and resourcefulness of its members. The ability among participants in this occupation to build a close knit community of self-sufficient farmers, raise children, and resist the police all at once is reflective of the MST's capacities and persistence on a national level. Over the course of the MST's twenty-six years of work, it has expropriated some thirty-five million acres, land that is now occupied by nearly 400,000 families.[6]

The settlements, which are often cooperatively organized (with some notable exceptions), are home to hundreds of MST-built schools, which have enabled tens of thousands of people to learn to read and write.[7] As the movement grew, it both carved its own autonomous social presence through direct action and became a major political force in Brazil. The ability of the movement to flex its grassroots muscles both outside the sphere of traditional politics and within the scope of the law, as well as pressure courts and politicians for change, makes the MST a particularly fitting movement to analyze in this book.

The MST began in 1984, when for four days in January, approximately a hundred landless farmers a met in the southern state of

Paraná. Because the organizers knew that the movement needed to be broad, landless leaders from thirteen different states were invited. This gathering was a break from the traditional land struggles, which had largely been led by unions. Many in large Brazilian labor unions believed the fight for agrarian reform should take place within union ranks—but unions didn't accept landless farmers as members. João Pedro Stédile, the Rio Grande do Sul Secretary of Agriculture at the time, along with other participants in the meeting, saw that the entire family of a landless farmer is affected by injustice, and therefore should be empowered to define what an alternative should look like. On that basis, Stédile believed they could incorporate the family into the movement. Thus, all members of the landless families were given rights to participate from the beginning of the MST. Besides empowering women outside of the traditional patriarchy, Stédile explained in 1999, "By including all members of the family, the movement acquires a remarkable potential force. Adolescents, for example, who are used to being oppressed by their fathers, realize that their votes in an assembly are as important as their fathers."[8] Over time, this breadth of membership contributed to the movement's longevity and strength in numbers when occupying land and creating objectives that take into account the needs of all family members.

The MST has been peacefully occupying unused land since 1985. When the activists take over land, in most cases they develop cooperative farms and build houses, schools, and health clinics on the land. They manage the land collectively in a sustainable way, as well as educate the children and advance gender equality.[9] As time passed, the MST started expanding their actions from simply taking over land, and began participating in marches, blockades, and occupations aimed at acquiring government assistance for their members, including improved access to credit, education, and healthcare. The MST actively fights against the use of genetically modified organisms (GMO) and industrial farming, while also working within their own camps to grow healthy food on a small-scale that generates employment for MST members.[10] Moving from its initial focus on land occupations, this diverse set of tactics and goals helped the movement remain flexible over time, and able to change with new agricultural practices and politics over the decades.

Brazil: Lula and the Landless   123

Among the reforms following the fall of the Brazilian dictatorship in 1985 was a new constitution written in 1988, establishing the right of the government to redistribute unused land to landless farmers. The land-reform measure established that all land must be used for the good of society. If land does not fulfill a social function, then the government reserves the right to take over and redistribute that land.[11] The institutional tool that carries out redistribution is the National Colonization and Agrarian Reform Institute (INCRA). Once INCRA certifies that land should be redistributed, the government appropriates it by paying the landowner for the land, and in the case of MST occupations, gives the title of the property to the landless farmers. The MST uses this process by pressuring the government and INCRA to follow their own legal procedures—first by occupying the unused land, and then by demanding ownership of that land, or land nearby the encampment.[12]

Unlike movements discussed in other chapters, the MST has remained an autonomous movement, lending tacit support to left-leaning regimes, but generally staying at the grassroots level. This has contributed to its longevity and effectiveness as a movement; it hasn't allowed itself to be coopted and undermined by allegiances to electoral politics like other movements in the region. The MST's actions are organized around building democratic, self-managed communities, while simultaneously pressuring the government to grant legal reforms.

Much of the MST's success lies in the democratic structures of its leadership, decision-making, and mobilization. Decisions and activities of the movement are debated in elected committees at various levels of the movement, ranging from the encampments to the regional offices. Within the MST, every member belongs to their own Base Group, a participatory committee that keeps power among the roots of the movement. The Base Groups in each encampment or settlement are made up of ten to twenty families, and each group has both a male and female coordinator.[13]

"That's our democracy," MST member João Amaral of Rio Grande do Sul, said of the Base Groups' process and general operations. Using consensus to arrive at decisions is an important part of the Base Groups' functionality, according to Amaral. "Perhaps that's one of the secrets of the unity of the MST. That we have not been divided over every issue where you have to make a decision. That's just it. We look for consensus, respecting the positions in the minority, until we arrive at consensus. There have been cases where positions which were at first in the minority became majority in the discussion process."[14]

This emphasis on a decentralized, bottom-up approach adds to the movement's sustainability and popularity among members. It is largely through the land occupations that MST leaders emerge; their skills are further developed in classes and meetings. The focus on bringing new leadership into the fold has spanned generations and undermines moves to centralize decision-making power in the hands of a few.

The actual occupation of land generates momentum and increases the number of MST members. Generally, once MST leaders decide on a parcel of unused land to occupy in a given area, they organize in the communities surrounding the land, describing the process INCRA goes through, and recruiting people to participate in the occupation. This community-based process brings people into the MST, incorporating participants into the necessary logistical tasks and preparation for the occupation, and then cementing relations through the solidarity that the occupation itself requires. After all of the planning is complete and the MST members decide to occupy the land, everyone is alerted at the last minute to maintain an element of surprise. Finally, participants enter the land, setting up their camp before dawn.[15] While this is a typical approach, over time MST members have also set up encampments in which people rotate through the camp during a two-to-five-year period as people are awarded land.

As Stédile explained in 2002,

On the night [of the occupation], the hired trucks arrive, well before daybreak, and go around the communities, pick up all they can carry and then set off for the property. The families have one night to take possession of the area and build their shelters, so that early the next morning, when the proprietor realizes what's happened, the encampment is already set up. The committee chooses a family to reconnoiter the place, to find where there are sources of water, where there are trees for shade.[16]

The goal is to remain in the fight in spite of any repression from police or thugs hired by the landowner: "[T]he main thing for a group, once it's gathered in an encampment, is to stay united, to keep putting pressure on the government."[17] The MST's persistence and technique of direct action has been incredibly successful over the years, and empowers its capacity to build an autonomous space for survival while pressuring the government at the same time.

After setting up camp, the group begins to push INCRA, court officials, and/or politicians for land. The activists often wait two to four years. In the meantime, landowners, their thugs, and police usually try to push the people off the land through harassment and assassinations. The organizational power of the MST, the solidarity of other groups that support it, and the dedication of settling families is decisive in whether or not the occupation will be successful.[18]

For many MST activists, life turns out to be better than what was suffered through before occupying the new land. Sonia Bergamasco, a professor of agrarian engineering at Campinas State University and the author of an MST settlement survey, said, "95 percent of people respond that they're better off now [after entering a settlement]. At least they have housing, they grow food and their kids go to school. Once they're settled, one of the first things communities do is start a school."[19]

The difficulty of life in the encampments pushes some to leave, but the adversity also brings MST members together. The living conditions are often tough in the camps, with plastic homemade tents to live in and poor water supplies. It is hard to remain healthy and prevent the spread of illness when an encampment is far from a hospital. To inspire solidarity, educate the children, and strengthen the will to stay in the fight, MST committees organize dances, soccer games, and theater performances.[20]

Pacote, an MST member, recalled,

We lost what little we had when we went to the encampment. We could take little even of those few things we owned into the new encampment, the only thing we took was our [wood-burning] cook stove. What little savings we had were soon gone, because we were earning nothing. We had no house or land to return to, no household goods, hardly any clothing, very few of our tools—everything was lost. And there was no way to go back and be the same person again to the old neighbors, the friends on the outside. Everything depended on the future and on the friends we had made in the encampment. There was no way back. [21]

In general, for people living in squalor or essentially enslavement as farm laborers, in slums, facing fierce poverty, drug addiction, crime, and lack of education and healthcare for their families, the MST encampments have been a clear improvement. Participating in the MST also means that they have control over their lives and a voice in the politics and direction of the country. [22]

At first, the MST's main focus was the fight for land. But quickly the activists discussed the need to educate their children to be able community members. The MST families wanted an empowering education for their children, so they could, "fight for their rights, to work together, to value the healthy life they could live in the country and to resist the lure of the city." The movement decided they needed to set up their own, more liberating education system. In 1990, they developed their aims for this system, which focused on training new leaders, showing the reality of society and how it can be changed, in addition to reading, writing, and analytical skills. Problems arose if children attending distant schools moved around a lot from camp to camp, and if the schools were outside, children were exposed to the elements. In response to such difficulties, MST activists set up itinerant schools in which teachers traveled with all of their supplies, including blackboards and desks. [23]

In March of 1998, when the police evicted MST members from a camp in Rio Grande do Sul, the activists decided to march to the state capital in protest. The itinerant schools went with them, operating in various settings along the march. One teacher described this educational experience:

Our desks and seats were the hard, cold ground, the blackboard was a piece of paper taped to the wall, to the railings, to the trees or just held in the teacher's hand. We learned by seeing, living, and doing. We calculated the kilometers, meters, centimeters of the road we had to take, the number of days it would take to arrive in the capital, what was produced in the towns we went through... We saw cars, horses, carts, trains, planes, a helicopter, boats, ships, so we studied means of transport. We sang in front of 2,000 people [at the teachers' union assembly in Porto Alegre]... When we decided to write a letter to the governor, we talked about the theme, we wrote about it, each one giving an idea, then it was read and approved by the collective school.[24]

This educational approach is illustrative of the MST's general focus on providing an alternative to the state and traditional Brazilian institutions. In the classroom, the farming fields, and the meetings, the MST has built its own world without waiting for the right election results, policy change, or political party backing; it has taken matters into its own hands to build the society it needs to survive and thrive.

"In whatever society, and even more so in Brazil, social change doesn't depend on the government but on the organization and the mobilization of society. It is the people that make the change," noted Stédile. "The people have to realize that it's useless looking to the government for everything. The government forms part of society and it's preferable that it's progressive... But the essential changes of society do not come from the government but from the energies that the working class succeeds in mobilizing when organizing for its rights."[25]

In this case, Stédile describes rights as something bestowed by states. At the same time, within the MST, the right for land is something that is acted upon without the state's blessing. The state cannot provide the inherent human right to land, but can block or deny that right— as can large land holders. A right, while potentially established and upheld through state legislation, can also be considered something one is born with, and thus entitled to, with or without the state's approval. The MST operates within this philosophy, while at the same time seeking to use the state as a tool for defense against land owners and repressive forces within the state itself, such as military and police who protect the interests of the agro-industry.

From the start of the movement, according to Stédile, the MST decided to remain autonomous from political parties. "Our analysis of the farmers' movements of Latin America and Brazil taught us that whenever a mass movement was subordinated to a party, it was weakened by the effects of inner-party splits and factional battles. It was not that we didn't value parties, or thought it was wrong to join them. But the movement had to be free from external political direction."[26] This belief has been put to the test with the movement's relations with the Workers Party.

The dance between the two forces has been different from other relationships in the region. For one thing, the massive size of the MST sets it apart from other South American movements, making it a formidable force and providing a model that others in the region have followed. The MST also uses the constitution and the state as a tool to meet its own goal: access to land. At the same time, the movement doesn't explicitly subordinate itself to political campaigns or the state. It is a model of a movement that engages the state, knowing the playing field, understanding the stakes, and moving ahead with a clear objective, democratic organization, and full understanding of the territory it is operating in and defending.

While other movements in Venezuela or Bolivia, for example, may bow down to politicians and parties during campaign seasons, and then prostrate themselves for government handouts or positions, the MST doesn't wait for the state—it acts according to its own logic and needs.

Lula and the Seizure of the Party by the State

The politics of Lula's party, his working-class background, and his decades-long commitment as a union organizer and advocate for Brazil's poor made him a popular presidential candidate among grassroots movements and activists in various elections. Yet his dramatic turn to the right upon taking office in 2003 had devastating effects on the working class in the country, and complicated his party's relationship with movements, particularly the MST. The power of the agro-industry, the need to expand the party's voter base, the limitations of working for change within the state, and the constraints placed on the presidency by global capitalism were some of the reasons for Lula's shift to the right. Over time, the hope inspired by Lula's election gave way to a sense of betrayal and a series of unique obstacles posed to movements dancing with the Brazilian state.

Lula was born into a poor family in 1945 in northeastern Brazil. When he was seven, his single mother, who worked as a laundress, put her eight kids into a cart and began the thirteen-day trip to the city of São Paolo to find work.[27] There, the teenaged Lula began working in a factory where he lost a finger in a machinery accident— a typical occurrence amidst the harsh working conditions. Lula's origins are among the working class he later helped organize for better conditions and wages.[28]

An influx of US investments in the auto industry in the 1960s and 1970s in Brazil, coupled with a migration of impoverished workers to cities due to droughts in the northeastern countryside, and a boom in the household appliance industry, all contributed to the rise of a new working class that empowered the labor movement. Lula quickly became a central leader in this movement, which won many victories despite harsh crackdowns during the dictatorship.[29] Brazil's dictatorship came to power in a military coup in 1964 and lasted until 1985, carrying out the torture and disappearances of political dissidents that was typical of South American regimes at the time.[30] During this crackdown, millions of workers went on strike against state-mandated wage controls. This and other strikes Lula led resulted in significant wage increases for workers, and helped pave the way to the end of the regime.[31]

When a March 1979 general strike called by the metal workers was declared illegal by the dictatorship, Lula responded, "They can declare the strike illegal, but it is just and legitimate, because its illegality is based on laws that weren't made by us and our representatives."[32] The Vila Euclides stadium in São Paolo was the only place that could hold the crowd of 80,000 attending a union rally and organizational meeting for the strike. Lula recalled the scene:

> When we [the union leaders] arrived, the fences, the stadium, the grass, everywhere was full of people, and the podium was only a little table. The sound system wasn't even big enough for a small

room, and I was alone, like a clown, on top of the table. Everyone
was getting tense, and the leaders were beginning to argue, because
the sound system wasn't any good and who knows what else was
wrong... You know what we did? We kept them there for four
hours on the field without a sound system... I yelled, the people in
front of me repeated what I'd said it was passed backwards... When
it started to rain, a few people started to leave. I shouted that no
one there would dissolve in the rain and nobody else went away.[33]

The PT grew out of this labor movement and brought together
a wide array of leftists, students, workers, and socialists. Its founding
manifesto states that its members sought "political independence"
and were "tired of serving as electoral fodder for politicians and parties representing the current economic, social, and political order...
Workers want to organize themselves as an autonomous political
force." It adds: "Participation in elections and parliamentary activities will be subordinated to the objective of organizing the exploited
masses and their struggles." Over the next two decades, the PT
would gradually grow to compete with other major parties. [34]

In the 1980s, though, the fortunes of the party waxed and waned.
Its initial populist rhetoric and radical objectives appealed only to
certain sectors of society. The party's eventual growth was tied to a
sense of discontent with traditional parties and neoliberal politics.
The PT was an alternative, and members of the party rode that alternative reputation into various political offices across the country.

In the 1989 presidential election, Lula received 44 percent of
the vote, and Fernando Collor de Mello won the presidency with
50 percent. But the economic crisis of the late 1990s hurt the PT as
its base of workers was hit hard by large unemployment rates. The
party grew, thanks in part to anger toward the neoliberal Fernando
Henrique Cardoso presidency, which lasted from 1994–2002.[35] Still,
in order to win the presidency, Lula and his allies in the PT knew
they had to expand their base beyond leftists and workers, and they
did so by making their policies more right-wing and seeking out
political allies on the right.

Lula and the PT had their eyes on the presidency, for the fourth
time, in the 2002 election. Lawyer and politician Ciro Gomes was

a candidate in this election, and became Lula's foremost opponent. Lula was portrayed in much of the Brazilian media as a radical until the lead-up to the 2002 election, when it became clear that he would build relationships with the right and make concessions in order to win votes. In previous elections, most of the PT party alliances were with smaller leftist parties. In the 2002 election season, however, Lula and the PT allied with central-right parties to win elections, abandoning the revolutionary plan he previously supported. The PT began to forge alliances with the Liberal Party (PL), whose José Alencar became Lula's vice-presidential running mate, and the Democratic Movement Party of Brazil (PMDB), which was part of the ruling coalition at the time.[36] The PT's shift from outsider to compromising coalition-builder was typical in other countries examined in this book as well, where candidates or parties moved away from their radical campaign platforms to build constrictive alliances with political parties that assured their electoral victories, but bound them to more conservative politics.[37]

When Lula rose in the polls in 2002, foreign investors and speculators punished the country, showing the power they had over Brazil. The result was that the *real* (Brazilian currency) lost a third of its value within three months.[38] In a response to this fear mongering, Lula announced that, if elected, he would maintain all of the financial policies of the previous governments: nothing would change, including in the areas of debt negotiations and finance regulation. With a new campaign advisor who had advised right-wing candidates, and alliances with right-wing party members, Lula expanded his support among voters and won the election with 61 percent of the vote.[39] The move to the right helped expand the number of PT supporters, but would have harsh consequences for the population. In the meantime however, immediately following his election, hope spread like wildfire among leftists across the country and the world.

"On election night, a sea of red flags lapped at the doors of the banks as thousands of supporters of the victorious PT waited for their hero, chanting campaign slogans," recounts the journalist Jan Rocha.

When [Lula] appeared on a giant screen making his acceptance speech, men and women wept with joy—and disbelief. Was this really happening? After thirteen years and three failed attempts at the presidency, was Luiz Inácio Lula da Silva really President of Brazil? Had the left wing finally come to power after 500 years of rule by the elite, the military, the landowners, the banks?[40]

Indeed, the left finally had come to power, but the PT's alliances with center-right and right-wing parties meant the left didn't have as much of a hold on the state as was initially believed. The PT depended on alliances with right-wing parties, and Lula appointed right-wing, neoliberal cabinet members, most infamously international corporate banker Henrique Meirelles as the president of the Central Bank. Meirelles had been previously in charge of FleetBoston Financial Group in the US, and he appointed an economic team that included neither leftists nor PT members.[41]

Shortly after taking office, Lula announced that his predecessor's agreement with the International Monetary Fund to prioritize debt payments would continue. He even went beyond what the IMF asked for regarding austerity measures. In an effort to direct government funds to pay the multi-billion dollar debt, he made a 45 percent budget cut which disproportionately affected social programs for the poor.[42] Lula's new plan taxed retirees in order to lower the social security deficit, limited workers' pensions, and lowered taxes for private investors.[43] In the resulting crisis, unemployment and poverty skyrocketed across the country. In May of 2003, unemployment reached 20.6 percent, a new record. These conservative economic moves angered those citizens hoping for larger structural changes in government.

Though Lula was elected on a leftist platform, he quickly unraveled the hope he had helped inspire among constituents, and distanced himself from the movements that helped put him in office. "Rather than the seizure of the state apparatus by the party, what took place was the seizure of the party by the state," Brazilian sociologist Francisco de Oliveira writes.[44] The PT was also struggling with a minority in Congress, holding only 91 of 513 seats during its first year in office. This weakened its power to enact the type of changes more radical members of the party sought.[45] In the hands of the state coopted PT party, Lula had betrayed the people, but he was also a victim of the state apparatus and the pressure of capitalist globalization. As in other countries, Lula's capitulation to neoliberal policies pre-empted the large, structural changes he promised as a candidate, and limited his actions to smaller social programs with restricted impact and no guarantee of longevity.

Members of the MST backed Lula at the ballot box in 2002 as part of an effort to lessen the extent to which the state supported large-scale agriculture and massive land holdings. "Now that we have a government that has been elected on a program of change, the latifúndio [landed estate] will also face the opposition of the government," Stédile said in an early 2003 interview. He was clear, however, that such a perceived change in the forces fighting against the landless was not enough to lead to agrarian reform. "The rhythm and the scale of agrarian reform will be determined by the capacity of the social movements to carry on organizing and mobilizing the poor in the countryside so that they struggle for agrarian reform."[46] It was this reliance on militant direct action, rather than uncritical support, which would define the MST's political relationship under Lula.

The Lula administration made some nods to the demands for agrarian reform. MST leader João Paulo Rodrigues admitted that "Lula has provided better supports for small farmers in the form of credit, technical assistance, education, electrification, and roads." But the actual redistribution of land under Lula has fallen short of his campaign promises. In fact, during his first term in office, land redistribution proceeded at a slower pace than it had under Cardoso.[47] In the face of Lula's betrayal, the MST didn't waver. In 2004, the MST occupied some 150 properties across the country. In May of 2005, 13,000 MST members marched to Brasilia to promote their demands.[48]

The MST never demanded to be a part of the new government. Instead, they chose to stand on the outside, pressuring the PT for land reform. The "government is like beans," member Juarez Santana Rocha pointed out. "It needs pressure to cook."[49] Specifically because it was autonomous from the party, the MST was not beholden to Lula, or the same political pressures the party faced. During the Lula's first administration, "The PT would pursue its Zero Hunger program and other social and economic initiatives and the MST would press the PT government for the structural reforms—like comprehensive agrarian reform—that it considered necessary," writes political science professor Harry Vanden. As an autonomous movement, the MST could continue to pursue its calls for radical changes. Remaining in the grassroots had paid off for the MST in terms of their credibility as a valid advocate for poor Brazilians. As distant and critical supporters of the PT, the MST was not associated with or tainted by the neoliberal shift of the Lula administration.[50]

Not only did Lula refuse to redistribute sufficient land to landless farmers, but he actively supported land large owners' use of toxic fertilizers, pesticides, and mono-crops like sugarcane, soybeans, and coffee for export. On the other hand, the MST has always advocated for the protection of small-scale-family and community farms, and called for agriculture without pesticides, or the use of GMO seeds (though pesticides and GMOs are also sometimes used by MST members). This all ran entirely counter to the country's massive agro-industry lobby and the Lula administration's stance.[51]

Lula's powerful support for agribusiness over small farms and landless farmers has been one of his biggest failures as an alleged "progressive." Thanks to Lula's encouragement, multinational agro-industrial corporations including Monsanto, ADM, Cargill, and Syngenta have expanded their operations throughout the country, increasing their ties with large landowners and Brazilian politicians. As political scientist Miguel Carter notes, "from 2003 to 2007, state support for the rural elite was seven times larger than that offered to the nation's family farmers, even though the latter represent 87 percent of Brazil's rural labor force and produce the bulk of food consumed by its inhabitants."[52] The result of this imbalance is an ever-growing landscape of endless seas of soy plantations, massive cattle ranches, and poisonous industrial farms that displace poor Brazilian families and cut down ever-larger swaths of rainforest while enriching the pockets of a handful of global elites.

The existing gross inequalities in land and wealth distribution were exacerbated by the policies of the Lula administration. In 2005, Cargill made $4 billion in income in Brazil alone. Ethanol production in the country skyrocketed, and in 2008, sugar cane production expanded by 14 percent, to cover 17 million acres. On the supply side, Monsanto maintains a very lucrative monopoly over pesticides and GMO seeds in Brazil. These sobering facts contrast sharply with the daily struggle to survive among poverty-stricken landless farmers and urban poor across the country.[53] Meanwhile, the unequal distribution of land in Brazil remained the norm. According to the MST in 2006, "the wealthiest 20 percent of the Brazilian population own 90 percent of the land, much of it being idle, used for ranching, tax write-offs, or to produce crops exclusively for export, while millions starve in the country."[54]

Lula's first years in office weren't completely without new programs to help impoverished sectors of the country. In 2006, Lula implemented the *Bolsa Familia* (Family Grant) program, targeting low-income families with social support including grants for food, education, and cooking gas—which impacted some eleven million families, approximately a quarter of the population. Yet the program was not applied alongside policies to address the key causes of poverty in the country, like the concentration of land and the unequal distribution of wealth.[55] When a future government decides to end the *Bolsa Familia* program, those eleven million families will be back where they started.

In 2006, voters re-elected Lula to the presidency, in part because he was the lesser of two evils. His opponent represented the most destructive forces of the right and elite. One editorial in the popular leftist weekly *Brasil de Fato* explained that, in spite of the enormous setbacks for the working class, voters should "properly distinguish between our principal enemy, our adversaries, and our allies. Wherever we get this wrong, we end up defeated… Thus, to vote for Lula, even with no illusions about his economic policy, is the duty of all of us who constitute the working and the Brazilian people."[56] And so members of the MST and other radical leftist movements and sectors in their country threw in their vote for Lula. But within the MST, this strategic electoral support did not direct energy away from direct action and radical organizing.

Years after Lula's initial election in 2002, many of his former grassroots supporters rightfully felt betrayed. However, the autonomy maintained by the MST has helped them remain an effective movement. Because of their distance from the PT, and their continued role as a self-directed organization, not subordinate to the party politics game, they have continued to empower their members to create better lives for themselves through direct action, and without having to bow down to the government.

In spite of government policies, the MST has succeeded in developing hundreds of farming cooperatives, one natural medicine factory, 1,600 government-recognized MST settlements, numerous health clinics, 1,800 primary and secondary schools for some 160,000 students, and a literacy program in which 30,000 adults participate. In 2005, the MST founded its own university outside of São Paulo.[57] After twenty-six years in operation, the MST has taken over roughly 35 million acres of land, settling nearly 400,000 families on titled land. In addition, 100,000 families continue waiting for land titles on occupied land.[58]

The dance between movements and governments in Brazil is unique to the extent that the MST has remained on the grassroots level, while the PT moved to the right. In other countries with leftist governments, the largest social movements have become more intertwined with political parties. In Bolivia, the MAS directly incorporates movements into its party and state machinery. In Venezuela, many of the grassroots programs and organizations making the Bolivarian process possible were, in part, created by the state. In Brazil, on the other hand, the MST remains totally separate from the Lula government and has broken relations with it. At the same time, it is also relatively easier for the government in Brazil to enact neoliberal policies because the movements are generally weaker compared to Bolivia, where a sharp turn to the right, like the one that Lula took, would generate major outcries and economically crippling actions from the movements.

At the state level, the trajectories, parties, and governments of Lula, Chávez, and Morales demonstrate important parallels. They all arrived in office due to popularity based on their humble backgrounds and progressive promises on the campaign trail. In the case of Bolivia and Venezuela, Morales and Chávez led constituent assemblies to rewrite their country's constitutions, paving the way for more certain institutional and social changes. The Brazilian government under Lula did not convoke such an assembly. Both Chávez and Morales nationalized powerful oil and gas industries to provide government funding for social and development programs, while Lula did not. Populist rhetoric, constitutional changes, and funds from nationalized industries cushion the setbacks in Venezuela and Bolivia.

The story of the MST and Lula illustrates the strategies of a movement that engages the state in a way that doesn't undermine the movement's objectives; the MST supported the lesser of two evils in the 2002 election, but did not stop occupying land when it became clear that Lula wouldn't grant the movement the land it needed at the speed required. The MST demonstrates the productive tactic of creating a broad movement that makes the revolution a part of everyday life, rather than a distant goal or illusive political party victory.

Landless farmers in Paraguay, a country to the south of Brazil, face challenges similar to their counterparts in the north. The rapidly expanding soy industry, coupled with a repressive state and right wing monopoly on power and military might, has threatened to wipe out the Paraguayan campesino entirely. While the landless movement in Paraguay is much weaker and smaller than the movement in Brazil, activists in Paraguay have taken a lot of inspiration and lessons from Brazil's MST, traveling to MST schools and conferences for classes and strategizing meetings. Like the MST, landless farmers in Paraguay have struggled against the expansion of the agro-industries and the repressive tactics of their government, working both with and against the presidency of Fernando Lugo, and autonomously fighting for their rights.

March in Asunción, Paraguay against pesticides and the soy industry's human rights violations. Sign says "Stop Fumigating Us: Justice for the Victims of the Pesticides." Photo by: Benjamin Dangl

CHAPTER SEVEN
Paraguay: Surviving Under the Red Bishop

In the morning in Asunción, Paraguay the trucks and buses took to the streets with a vengeance, making up for the night's lost time. The smell of fresh bread mixed in the air with the pungent aroma of burning garbage. Dogs paced their yards and driveways behind fences, dreaming and going insane. Butterflies hovered lazily, bewildered in the exhaust-choked trees. As the sun baked the streets, the ancient buses rumbled on like monsters, urban dragons trapped in the wrong century.

Each bullet hole on the downtown light posts tells a story. Some of them are from civil wars decades ago, some from successful and unsuccessful coups, others from police crackdowns. The size of the hole, the angle of the ricochet, all tell of an escape, a death, another dictator in the palace by the river.

On May 1, 2009, a few blocks from one particularly bullet-hole-ridden post, a crowd gathered to protest the lack of justice for human rights abuses by the Alfredo Stroessner dictatorship. Stroessner was a despotic leader whose ghost haunts every political rally in Paraguay. He ruled the country with an iron fist from 1954–1989, directing the torture and disappearance of thousands of political dissidents. Though this gathering of people originally convened to commemorate International Workers Day, leaders shifted the focus of speeches from labor issues after receiving news of the early morning arrival of an exiled Interior Minister from the Stroessner regime.

Just hours before the rally began, eighty-six-year-old Sabino Augusto Montanaro arrived in Paraguay for the first time after twenty years of self-imposed exile in Honduras, where he lived to avoid prosecution for war crimes. As Minister of the Interior, Montanaro played a key role in orchestrating an intricately planned and documented system of torture and murder under the Stroessner dictatorship. Paraguayan bishop Mario Melanio Medina said that Montanaro was Stroessner's "right hand man" and "number one [in command] after Stroessner."[1] Despite facing numerous criminal charges

139

in his home country, the wheelchair-bound Montanaro returned in part because, as his lawyer told reporters, "according to Paraguayan law, he is too old to go to jail."[2] His confidence in his impunity from punishment was yet one more slap in the face of the Paraguayan human rights movement. In 2006, Stroessner himself died at age ninety-three in Brazil without being tried for his crimes.[3]

Back at the May 1 rally, the city sweltered in the mid-morning heat, and some 1,000 protesters began marching toward the private clinic where Montanaro had arrived after his early morning flight. While pounding drums and yelling political chants, the marchers paraded down the middle of many central city streets that were empty due to the holiday. The chants and drumming increased in volume when the marchers passed the red headquarters of the Colorado Party—Stroessner's party—which lost its sixty-year grip on the country with the 2008 election of former bishop Fernando Lugo.

The march reached a climax when it arrived at the clinic. Dozens of riot police had already surrounded the building, creating a wall with their thick metal shields, while hundreds of victims and family members of victims of Montanaro's repression rallied in the streets outside, demanding justice. When the majority of the marchers arrived at the clinic, one group charged the front door, trying to break through the police line and get inside. The police began beating the protesters with clubs, leaving one man bloody and stunned. News spread that Montanaro was going to be taken to a military hospital, and protesters began to surround a back exit to the clinic. When the large wooden doors opened to let the van through, protesters lunged at the ambulance carrying Montanaro, tossing rocks and shattering a side window of the vehicle. Police crashed their night sticks on the activists, dispersing the crowd with a wave of rubber bullets.

The shadow of the dictatorship hangs over Paraguay in more ways than one. Beyond the physical manifestation evident in the return of Montanaro are its lasting psychological and political impacts. Though the Colorados lost the 2008 elections, this monstrous party's legacy still maintains its political power. The state apparatus was largely expanded under the Colorado party, and the justice system was transformed into a tool for the defense of the oligarchy and the persecution of anyone who stood in the party's way.

On the surface, the election of Lugo broke with the country's repressive history. His leadership has shown, however, that the same institutions, people, and companies wield the same power in Paraguay, and Lugo is not willing to confront that status quo. The first year of his administration proved that not only would he allow previous repressive policies to continue, but he would enable them to expand their reach, while continuing to repress and criminalize the very human rights and campesino movements that helped bring him to power.

In the years following the Stroessner era, new interests have pushed their way into Paraguayan electoral politics. According to Paraguayan political analyst Tomas Palau, current powerful interests in the country can be divided into four groups: 1) The oligarchy, consisting of soy growers and cattle ranchers who depend on paramilitaries to allow them to expand, 2) The narco-traffickers who pay off politicians, 3) The lumpen business class, which relies on international trade and black market goods,[4] and 4) the transnational corporations that buy and export soy, cotton, and sugar. According to Palau, political parties are simple transmitters of those interests.[5] Meanwhile, poor urban and campesino movements are sidelined and repressed by this concentrated political power.

The Oligarchy's New Face

Partly because of his life history, the bishop Fernando Lugo appeared ready and willing to confront these interest groups. He was born in 1951 and as a young man taught in a rural school district. In 1977, Lugo was ordained as a Catholic priest and worked as a missionary in Ecuadorian indigenous communities until 1982. He then spent ten years studying at the Vatican, at which time he was appointed head of the Society of the Divine Word in Paraguay. In 1994, he became the bishop of the Paraguayan diocese of San Pedro. Though Lugo was frequently away from Paraguay, he did not avoid the repercussions of the Stroessner dictatorship and its conservative influence. In fact, three of his brothers were exiled, and the conservative Catholic hierarchy pressured Lugo to resign as bishop due to his support for landless families' settlements on large estates owned by absent elites. He resisted this pressure until his name began to circulate as a presidential candidate. Old Paraguayan laws, stemming from anti-Jesuit legislation passed hundreds of years ago, forbid members of the clergy from running for president. In 2007, Lugo's resignation as bishop allowed him to realize his ambitions as a presidential contender.[6]

As president, the "Red Bishop" (a nickname referring to his supposed leftist politics on the campaign trail) became the leader of one of the most corrupt nations in the world, a country marked by catastrophic inequalities. Forty percent of the population own just 11.5 percent of the wealth, while the wealthiest 10 percent control 40.9 percent. Lugo hasn't shown the capacity to confront this inequality. However, as the soy industry and its penchant for violence against small farmers threaten to wipe out the Paraguayan campesino entirely, many communities are fighting back—with or without Lugo's backing.

Though Lugo won the election, the right-wing opposition still ended up controlling 82 percent of the senate and the lower house.[7] While much of the government remains in the hands of the right, a significant amount of Lugo's party's base lies with the popular sectors of the country. Yet the administration has all but squandered any chance of a productive relationship with them. Many landless and small farmers around the country have been demanding that the government conduct a new land survey to assess which lands were seized by Stroessner and illegally given to friends of the dictatorship, and which could therefore be legally redistributed to landless farmers. The rural movements' other main demand is to stop the massive destruction of the environment and the campesino way of life through the use of paramilitary actions and poisonous pesticides on the soy crops of industrial farms.[8]

Under Lugo, the economic inequality, deficit in democracy, and marginalization of movements and dissenting voices has been maintained, albeit with a president who represented more of a "populist" veneer than his predecessors. This contradiction has aided the right and confused and aggravated Lugo's voter base. Paraguayans have sought to make sense of Lugo's betrayal in various ways.

Leticia Galeano, a young, short-haired Paraguayan activist, understands the hopes and failure of the Lugo administration, as she's been involved with this process from the grassroots for years through the Popular Agrarian Movement (MAP) of Paraguay. Her father is a key MAP leader and she grew up in a community that was destroyed by soy production and later reclaimed by the same community of activist-farmers. In April of 2009, we met at a restaurant serving traditional Guaraní dishes, with folk music playing in the background. "Repression has stayed the same under Lugo because of the justice system," said Galeano. "In general everything is the same as before. The same system of repression is in place... Lugo is very limited in what he can do, but people are still hopeful about Lugo and he still has a lot of support." This enthusiasm is based on a consideration of the alternative: a more repressive right-wing administration.[9]

Galeano believed the movements were pressuring the government, but were still orienting themselves to the new challenge of having a supposed ally in office. The government wasn't responding to pressure from below, she explained. "There are very many obstacles to the collaboration with the government. There is no change because the government and Lugo have no interest in changing things. Lugo says he wants land reform, and meets with social organizations, and talks about change. But doesn't do anything." Galeano mainly blames Lugo's inability to create change on his lack of political allies. "He's too isolated to make changes," she said, "He is all alone at the top." With explicitly right-wing parties controlling the House and Senate, any progressive changes are stifled. But Lugo has hands tied in other areas as well.

In order to win the presidency, Lugo had to make a series of contradictory promises, on the one hand to center and right-wing politicians and parties for their alliances and support, and on the other hand to the leftist and grassroots movements for their votes and campaign militancy. Hence the disappointment, a year into his administration, when these contradictions manifested themselves in his politics and positions. But in Paraguay—unlike other countries where movements are perhaps more experienced in dealing with potential allies in power—many movements and organizations were disoriented one year after Lugo assumed office. Many understood the stakes and new political context, but were unsure about how to proceed.

"It's good for the oligarchy if Lugo stays in power and does nothing," Galeano noted. "And people are uncertain because they know that if they fight against Lugo, they are giving space to the right. No one knows what route to take, though they understand the situation. Organizations, leftist parties all understand, but they still don't know what to do with a Lugo government. It's different from before, but now they're in a difficult situation." The situation of Paraguayan social movements is another example of the fact that it can be simpler to be totally against the government—as was the case for Paraguayans in the past—than negotiating with a quasi-ally in power. "We know we won't win much by supporting him, but we'll lose everything without him. So it's important to be very strategic now," Leticia concluded as we finished sharing our manioc flour pancakes.

Defending a self-described leftist government just for the sake of preventing the right from taking power has a demobilizing effect, but it also has an undeniable appeal for those who understand the death and destruction wielded by the right and the past dictatorship. An isolated and traumatized country, with an incredibly strong oligarchy and without a free press, has a different set of odds than those confronted by movements in other countries. In the political terrain of Paraguayan agriculture, the dance between the state and the movements has had particularly devastating results for campesinos.

The Land Lugo Promised

Thousands of Paraguayan farmers raised their clubs, fists, and placards into the air while marching through the streets of Asunción on March 25, 2010. The farmers demanded that Lugo follow through on his campaign promise of agrarian reform, including the distribution of land to poor farmers, and access to health care, education, better homes, and roads for rural communities. After a year and a half in office, Lugo's failures to meet such demands have led various farmer organizations to directly oppose his administration.

National Campesino Federation (FNC) general secretary Odilón Espínola said that Lugo has continued the "same discourse [as previous presidents] and has not followed through on his promises to realize agrarian reform." Though Paraguay became a democracy following the end of the dictatorship in 1989, Espínola said that "no government has responded to the needs of the campesinos."[10]

Campesino leader Marcial Gómez told Reuters that if the demands of the marchers were not met, campesino movements would have to resort to their standard strategies of direct action. Without a response from Lugo, "We don't have any other choice but to resort to other means used in our historic struggle, such as the occupation of lands and the blockading of highways, if we want to obtain a small piece of land to work on."[11] Gómez's sentiment and anger reflected a larger impatience among campesinos across the country.

In the face of such pressure, Lugo has been conciliatory only in rhetoric. In September of 2008, when speaking of negotiations between his administration and the landless farmer movement, he said, "I think that as long as there is a will to sit down and talk, using the tool of dialogue, and work out consensuses, then it's possible for us, ourselves, to design an integrated land reform that would benefit the majority of landless peasant farmers one finds in Paraguay."[12] But Lugo has shown neither the will to seriously negotiate nor the ability to develop a functional plan for land reform.

Paraguayan human rights lawyer and activist Orlando Castillo explained that the unofficial agricultural objective of the Lugo administration, which follows the strategy of his predecessors, is to evacuate the rural area of campesinos and push them into the city, thus allowing for even more uninhibited growth of the large-scale agro-industry. This vision is in direct conflict with the traditional Paraguayan family-based farm model. Lugo's security strategy, Castillo explained, "is to create this idea that insecurity and social strife doesn't come from the soy industry or the displacing force of the agro-industry, but that the public enemies are actually those who are in fact the victims of this system, and who are painted as criminals and repressed." When the rural poor are construed as the public enemy, displaced from the countryside and then forced to live in urban slums, the actual underlying problems that lead to poverty are ignored. The emphasis is on security and repression, thus expanding the levels of poverty and displacement in the country.[13]

This cycle is reflected in Paraguay's national statistics. A report from the Paraguayan Human Rights Coordinator (CODEHUPY), states that in 2007, Paraguay exported more than 4.3 million tons of soy and $370 million in beef. Between 2007 and 2008, the soy industry grew by 26 percent. Meanwhile, 600,000 children in the county remain malnourished. Seventy-seven percent of the fertile land in the country is owned by one percent of the population, while the small farmers that make up 40 percent of the population own just 5 percent of the farmland. Diego Segovia, a researcher who contributed to the CODEHUPY report explained that "Campesino families cannot possibly compete on the market with the small quantities that they produce."[14] In addition, the toxic, militarized, and ever-growing nature of agro-industry doesn't even allow for small farmers to produce for their own consumption.

While the odds facing contemporary campesino movements are huge and complicated by the contradictory positions of the Lugo administration, movements in the country have been fighting against this inequality for decades, with mixed results. The campesino social movements in Paraguay that survived the dictatorship reemerged after the return to democracy in 1989. Many campesino organizers suffered severe repression under the dictatorship and, throughout the 1990s, were able to reorganize their strategies to suit the new situation of the country and expand their networks. Some of these organizations focused on local issues, defending the rights and livelihoods of their members, while others had more regional or national objectives. The need for unity among the campesino organizations nationwide has been a recurring theme among rural organizers for decades.[15]

Toward the end of the 1990s, campesino demands began to revolve around issues dealing with socio-political structures beyond their own immediate area and lives, and engaged the national system that they saw as connected to their own local struggles. As campesino leader Eladio Flecha noted in 2000, "We have realized that the agrarian problems are not restricted just to the countryside, and to the campesino, but are national problems, to the point that the agrarian crisis has repercussions in other sectors."[16] Though the campesinos may have shifted their focus toward demanding structural changes from the state, they remain marginalized, while the real political power resides with the state—a decidedly repressive structure and a continuation of the Colorado Party and Stroessner legacy.

Historically, the relation between campesino movements and the state has been based on conflict and tension. Many campesino organizations view the state as a political adversary—particularly when the Colorado Party was in power for so long—but also as a mechanism that opposes, coopts, and demobilizes the movements and their demands. Nonetheless, while movements may maintain an anti-state discourse throughout their actions and campaigns, the Paraguayan state has historically remained the primary receiver and manager of campesino demands and proposals.[17]

A Different Kind of Terrorism

On September 24, 2008, when Lugo spoke at the UN for first time, he denounced soy industry as a type of "terrorism which in my country affects the children who are dying from pesticides."[18] An estimated twenty million liters of agrochemicals are sprayed across Paraguay each year.[19] But the President has yet to follow up with any plans to combat that terrorism. Paraguay is the fourth largest producer of soy in the world, and soy makes up 40 percent of Paraguayan exports and 10 percent of the country's GDP.[20] Indeed, this rapidly expanding industry has terrorized small farmers.

Managing the gargantuan agro-industry in South America are transnational seed and agro-chemical companies including Monsanto, Pioneer, Syngenta, Dupont, Cargill, Archer Daniels Midland (ADM), and Bunge. International financial institutions and development banks have promoted and bankrolled the agro-export business of monoculture crops—much of Paraguayan soy goes to feed animals in Europe. The profits have united political and corporate entities from Brazil, the US, and Paraguay, and increased the importance of Paraguay's cooperation with international businesses.

In Paraguay especially, the expansion of the soy industry has occurred in tandem with violent oppression of small farmers and indigenous communities who occupy the vast land holdings of the wealthy. Most rural Paraguayans cultivate diverse subsistence crops on small plots of ten to twenty hectares, but do not have titles to their land nor do they receive assistance from the state.[21] The Paraguayan government has historically represented the soy growers in this conflict by using the police and judicial system to punish campesino leaders. Protests have been portrayed and treated as crimes, and campesino leaders have been characterized as delinquents, and linked to kidnappings and a supposed guerilla movement with ties to Colombian guerilla groups.[22] A report compiled by the Paraguayan arm of the international human rights organization the Peace and Justice Service (SERPAJ) concluded "that with public forces in its hands, the alliance of the Public Prosecutor and the Supreme Court, which guarantees impunity, has created a campaign of massive repression of the campesino sector, in order to facilitate and guarantee the expansion of genetically modified soy in the country."[23]

Since the 1980s, national military and paramilitary groups connected to large agribusinesses and landowners have evicted almost 100,000 small farmers from their homes and fields and forced the relocation of countless indigenous communities in favor of soy fields. While more than a hundred campesino leaders have been assassinated, only one of the cases was investigated with results leading to the conviction of the killer. In the same period, more than two thousand other campesinos have faced trumped-up charges for their objections to the industry.

The vast majority of Paraguayan farmers have been poisoned off their land either intentionally or as a side effect of the hazardous pesticides dumped by soy cultivation in Paraguay every year. Beginning in the 1990s, as farmers saw their animals die, crops withering, families sickening, and wells contaminated, most packed up and moved to the city.[24] The havoc wreaked by agro-industries has created some of the most grave human rights violations since Stroessner's reign. Press reports say that "school classes are often cancelled on days of crop spraying on the field twenty meters away because the children faint from the smell."[25]

A report produced by the Committee of Economic, Social, and Cultural Rights of the United Nations stated that "the expansion of the cultivation of soy has brought with it the indiscriminate use of toxic pesticides, provoking death and sickness in children and adults, contamination of water, disappearance of ecosystems, and damage to the traditional nutritional resources of the communities."[26] A social investigation carried out in 2007 found that, in the four departments where soy production is the highest, 78 percent of families in rural communities near soy fields showed health problems caused by the frequent crop spraying in the soy fields, 63 percent of which are due to contaminated water.[27]

In May of 2009, campesinos from the around the country gathered at an office of the National Workers Center to explain how the soy industry and pesticides were ruining campesino life. In a mixture of the widely-spoken indigenous Guaraní language and Spanish, many of the speeches from mothers, fathers, and children reflected views I had heard around the country. According to the people at this meeting, the very existence of campesino life in Paraguay is at stake. They called for the unification of disparate unions and organizations to combat the soy industry. Lugo's presidency seemed to offer a new dilemma to the group; they were unsure about how to combat this supposed comrade in the presidency. Very few of the elected officials invited attended the testimonials; noticeably absent was the Minister of Agriculture. Most of the campesino speakers didn't even talk about Lugo, they talked about the system—the businesses and institutions that still maintain power regardless of who occupies the presidency.

Following the discussions, participants in the gathering took to the streets in a march. People came prepared to paint skulls and cross bones on the pavement and denounce the various organizations and offices they stopped at along the protest route. Some activists were dressed in the suits recommended for use when spraying pesticides—suits campesinos living next to soy fields couldn't afford or wear every day in the stifling heat.

During the march, I spoke with Alvino Jara, President of the Campesino Organization of Simón Bolívar. He wore mirrored sunglasses and told me, "We are traditionally organic producers, and the soy business owners want us to plant genetically modified transgenic soy instead. They've already planted a thousand hectares of their own crops and are pressuring us to leave. They threaten us with armed men that pass through the community without any oversight from the police." He spoke of areas in his community that used to have rich lakes, full of fish the locals ate. The lake is shrinking because the soy farmers use so much of it for irrigating their own massive crops.

"Now all the fish are dead," he pointed out. "The lake's water level is much lower, and it is bad water now. All of it is contaminated."

Very present at this march was the community of Tekojoja, home of the growing Popular Agrarian Movement (MAP) of Paraguay. It is a place that has faced enormous repression from the soy farmers and their thugs, and led a legendary resistance against them, producing many campesino leaders. A visit to this community provided insight into the horrible history of the soy industry in Paraguay, the state's collusion with soy producers, and the possibilities within the people's power of organizing and resisting in the face of enormous odds.

Resistance in a Sea of Soy

The first of several buses we would take from Asunción toward Tekojoja heated up like a sauna as polka played on the radio. Hawkers came on the bus selling sunglasses, radios, and pirated DVDs. Particularly dedicated salesmen gave impassioned speeches about the superior characteristics of their product, pushing samples onto the unwilling and bored passengers. One sales pitch promised that garlic pills could cure insomnia and cancer.

We passed countless fields of soy and Cargill silos, but also vegetable stands from small farmers and simple roadside restaurants where people could escape into the shade with a cold beer. The dirt road from Caaguazú toward Tekojoja was a rutted expanse of churning red sand; it took us three hours to travel 50 kilometers. The bus fought its way over the deep potholes, the engine reaching a fevered pitch, and every one of its metal bones rattling along with those of its passengers.

That same night, we arrived in Tekojoja and went to Gilda Roa's house, a government-made structure without running water. A land and farmer rights activist, Roa's shirt portrayed plants breaking through a bar code. Inside her house, the walls were covered with anti-soy and anti-GMO posters. She pulled up plastic chairs for us in front of the garden with bright stars as a backdrop, and began talking. Roa spent 2000–2002 in Asunción studying to be a nurse, and had worked as one in a nearby town. Now she dedicates her life to activism in her community. As Paraguayan folk music played on the radio, and moths bounced around the lights, Roa told us the story of her community.[28]

Tekojoja stands on land given to campesinos as part of a Public Land Reform Program. In the 1990s, Brazilian soy farmers—with armed thugs, lawyers, and political connections to protect them—gradually expanded onto the community's land, forcing a series of violent evictions of the farming families.[29] In 2003, the MAP began to recover the lands taken from them by Brazilians, but corrupt judges and the mercenaries hired by soy producers kept pushing the farmers off their land.[30]

Large-scale Brazilian soy farmers are often viewed by small-scale Paraguayan campesinos as an imperialist threat. This perception is tied up into a sense of Paraguayan nationalism against foreigners, but is also connected to the fact that most of the massive soy plantations are run by Brazilians who have built entire communities of clear-cut soy plantations and Brazilian towns deep in what used to be Paraguayan forests and small farmers' land. The anger against Brazilian soy farmers is also based on the fight to survive against the challenges of the industry. Paraguayans often refer to Brazilians in sweeping, condemning statements when describing their struggle for land.

On December 2, 2004, Brazilian land owners accompanied by police burned down numerous houses and farmland in Tekojoja as part of an eviction process. A statement from the MAP described this brutal act:

> [A]fter the tractors destroyed our crops, they came with their big machines and started immediately to sow soy while smoke was still rising from the ashes of our houses. The next day we came back with oxen and replanted all the fields over the prepared land. When the police came, we faced them with our tools and machetes. There were around seventy of us and we were ready to confront them. In the end they left.[31]

The campesinos' houses and crops were destroyed and they had no assurances that the Brazilians would not orchestrate another eviction. Still, as most had no place to go, the community members decided to persevere, staying on the land and fighting for legal recognition as the owners. Roa explained, "We planted seeds with fear as we didn't know if our crops would be destroyed. And we began to reconstruct the houses." But again at 4 a.m. on June 24, 2005, the Brazilians and police attacked the community. "They arrested children, blind people, old men, and pregnant women, everyone, throwing them all in a truck." Roa said. "They threw gas and oil on the houses, burning them all down as the arrests went on."

In this standoff between the thugs, police, and unarmed campesinos, two farmers, who the Brazilians mistakenly identified as MAP leaders and brothers Jorge and Antonio Galeano, were killed by gunfire. One of the victims was Angel Cristaldo Rotela, a 23 year-old who was about to be married, and had just finished building his own home the day before the police burned it to the ground. The wife of Leoncio Torres, the other victim, was left a widow with eight children. To this day, the people who committed the crimes have not faced justice.

After the murders, campesinos and activists from around the country rallied in support of Tekojoja, supplying the besieged community members with tarps and food. Finally, the Supreme Court ruled that the land should go to the local farmers, and as part of the reparations for the violence the community suffered, President Nicanor Frutos commissioned the building of forty-eight homes, but without water or sewage connection at the time of this writing.

The plight of Tekojoja sheds light on the situation many farming communities are finding themselves in across Paraguay. While the residents of Tekojoja remain on their land, many others are forced to flee to slums in the city as soy producers push them off their land. Roa explained this cycle of displacement:

> When the small farmers are desperate, and the pesticides are hurting them, there is no money, and so they sell their land for a little money, which is more than they've ever had, thinking that life in the city will be better, easy—but it's not so easy. A lot of people who end up gathering garbage in the city are from the countryside. They don't know how to manage their money, so for example, they'll spend all their money on a used, broken-down car first, and then end up in the city broke, without any jobs or place to stay.

The victory of Tekojoja was due to the tenacity of the farmers who refused to leave their land for the false promise of rich city life. Now, Roa believes that through strong organizational skills they can continue to resist any pressure. But their fight is far from over. Though they tore the soy plants out of their land, residents live sandwiched between seemingly limitless expanses of soy, and they, their animals, and their crops continue to suffer from exposure to toxic pesticides.

By dawn the next day, most of Roa's neighbors were already up, getting to work before the sun made labor unbearable. Chickens milled about houses, the red dirt yards were still damp from the night's dew, and radios tuned in to a community radio station mixing music with political commentary in Guaraní. A neighboring community activist invited us to his house to start the day with Paraguayan's essential beverage, yerba maté served hot in the morning and specially prepared with coconut and rosemary. We sat in his kitchen as the sun streamed through the cracks between the boards in the wall, illuminating ribbons of smoke from the fire, while his children and pigs played on the dirt floor.

An ominous presence loomed over this bucolic scene. The neighboring Brazilian soy farmers had already shown up with their tractors, spraying pesticides on nearby crops. I could smell the chemicals in the air already. We walked toward the fields until the sweet, toxic odor grew stronger. We passed one tractor very closely as clouds of the pesticides drifted toward us. I began to feel a disorienting sensation of dizziness and nausea. My eyes, throat and lungs burned and my head ached, something the locals go through on a daily basis. The physical illness caused by the pesticides contributes to breaking down the campesino resistance.

I am reminded that this is a surrounded community, not just because of the soy crops that circle these islands of humanity, or the pesticides that seep into every water source, crop, and conversation, but also because the Brazilian soy farmers live next to and drive through these impoverished communities with total impunity, and with the windows of their shiny new trucks rolled up tightly. Mounted somewhat precariously on the back of a few mopeds, we bounced along the dirt roads, which petered out into paths to

another cluster of homes. On our way there, we passed one Brazilian who glared at us until we were out of sight. Roa knew him: he
had participated in the razing and burning of their homes. The fact
that he was still free added insult to injury. And if the locals were to
accuse him, said Roa, or even yell at the Brazilian murderers, police
would show up and haul them off to jail. "This is the hardest part,"
she explained. "That we see them and can't do anything."

The moped rolled to a stop in front of Virginia Barrientos'
home, a few miles from Roa's, directly bordering a soy field. The
land Barrientos lived on for the past four years is a peninsula jutting
into the sea of soy. She occupied her land, which used to be covered
with soy, in February of 2005 and won legal ownership to it. But life
since gaining the land has been far from easy; pesticides have terrorized her family since they moved there.

"Just before we harvest our food the Brazilians will spray very
powerful pesticides," Barrientos explained. "This spraying causes the
headaches, nausea, diarrhea we all suffer." Her thin children were
gathered with her on the porch of the home. "There are a lot of
problems with the water," she continued. "When it rains, the pesticides affect our only water source." She spoke with us while breast-
feeding her baby as chickens pecked at peanuts in the yard, and her
children stared at us with wide eyes. They were in a desperate situation. "We can't go anywhere else," she said.[32]

Barrientos said the pesticides affected her plants and animals as
well, making some of the crops that do actually grow taste too bitter
to eat. Her pigs' newborn babies died, and the chickens were ill. Part
of the problem, she pointed out, is that the Brazilian soy farmers
intentionally choose to fumigate during strong winds which blow the
poison onto her land. We passed dead corn stalks on the way to her
well, which she insisted on showing us. It was located at the end of
a long field of soy, so that the runoff from the field dripped into the
well, concentrating the pesticides in her only water source. The family lives in a poisoned misery, while the soy producer responsible for
it lives in comparative luxury away from his fields.

Isabel Rivas, a neighbor of Barrientos' with a big smile and
loud laugh in spite of her grim living situation, told us, "When we
drink the water we can smell the chemicals. It turns out they were

washing the chemical sprayers in our source of water, in a little stream nearby."[33]

The forces threatening Tekojoja are also the forces destroying many other communities throughout the Paraguayan countryside. The expansion of this industry takes place with the support of the Paraguayan state, military, and justice system. The fusion of corporate and state power directed at the rural campesinos is typical of other countries as well, particularly as soy expands in Brazil, Argentina, and across South America. In Paraguay, however, the situation is exacerbated by the historically repressive machinery of the state, distinctive due to the long term reign of Stroessner and his party's stranglehold on the political culture of the country.

Facing this combination of odds, the Paraguayan campesinos' dance with the state is further undermined by Fernando Lugo's facade of populism; by portraying himself rhetorically as an advocate and defender of the poor while upholding the neoliberal system and Colorado-style repression, he has ironically become one of the best allies of the political right and soy industry. Though touted as a victory for democracy, Lugo's electoral success against the Colorado Party's leadership has tragically proven to be just what the oligarchy needed to maintain their hold on power. With Lugo as a puppet for the right, the infrastructure of repression, exploitation, and centralization of power can continue as it has, but with a different face. How the country's movements address this challenge in the coming years will define their existence, and determine the fate of the country's disappearing campesinos.

"Without community organizing nothing works"

The media portrays the rapidly expanding neighborhood of Los Bañados ("The Bathed Place," named because the Paraguay River often rises up and washes the houses and the land of its residents away), as a place of desperate poverty and violent crime. Many Paraguayans wouldn't dream of traveling to this sprawling community between downtown Asunción and the river. But while many of the displaced people from the Paraguayan countryside end up impoverished in the slums of the nation's cities, this is one neighborhood in

Asunción that has risen up to manage its own destiny, pressure the government for funding and support, fight poverty, and build community from the ground up.

Creedence Clearwater Revival played on the stereo in the streets where the Bañado Sur neighborhoods of San Juan and Santa Cruz meet. This river-shore community had a livelier street culture than any other I had seen throughout Asunción. Children played, neighbors shared iced tea on the stoops of their homes and in front of corner stores, fishermen walked past with poles and their recent catches in buckets. The main road is made of dirt and the monstrous buses that roar through the city streets don't venture into this comparatively serene neighborhood.

Human rights lawyer Orlando Castillo, who was born and raised in the Bañados, spoke of the differences between the social fabric and activity in the Bañados *versus* the rest of the city.

> In Los Bañados people return at 6 p.m. and carry on with their social life, on the soccer pitch or at the social center. There are communal spaces and there is interaction, there are strong links, arguments, and solidarity. On the contrary, in the peripheries of the city the people get home at 9 p.m. and lock themselves in their house. The poverty is the same, but there are not strong relationships among neighbors.[34]

Local resident activist Carmen Castillo (Orlando's sister) spoke about how her community developed an organization called the Coordinating Committee of Community Defense (CODECO) to defend the neighborhood's rights, and address poverty and unemployment. They work to improve homes, apply for grants, deal with issues related to access to water, electricity, and healthcare. She said that they don't receive municipal help for their neighborhood—the roads and all forms of infrastructure are made by the people and international aid organizations. "The state doesn't exist here," she said. "We organize projects to make money and organize raffles, soccer games, and so on." CODECO is made up of 10 different neighborhoods and involves around five thousand people. Through it, residents of the Bañados have resisted displacement, gentrification, and flooding over the years. At the same time, their struggles have pushed them together as an organization.[35]

A CODECO meeting I attended provided insight into how the organization works on the ground. First of all, most of the participants at the meeting were women, and they participated more than the men—a sight rarely seen in many of the political meetings I've attended across the continent. They discussed recycling programs, security in the neighborhood, and what to get for food for an upcoming new member meeting and training session. Representatives discussed trips to be made to Cuba for surgery, as part of Mission Milagros, a program open to Paraguayans for eye surgery. The meeting seemed to be a kind of popular mayor's office, in which participating residents were able to make decisions directly due to the absence of the state.

Through this process of self-management and advocacy on behalf of the residents' rights and needs, CODECO leaders have been able to rehabilitate their own health center and hire health professionals to work in the neighborhood—a place doctors often refuse to visit. "We have our own capable people in our sector who know the neighborhood, and if no one else wants to come here we'll use our own people," Castillo said. After the meeting, she explained to me that the locals planted all the trees and plants in the neighborhood, providing much needed shade as well as protecting the area from floods. The community takes care of its security in an unconventional way as well. Castillo noted, "Real security is caring for your community, knowing your neighbors; community organizing fights crime."

Another example of this solidarity emerges when someone in the community is sick. When a neighbor becomes ill or needs medical care and is lacking funds, the neighbors get food together, have a barbecue, and sell the food to benefit their neighbor. Similar cooperation takes place with the building of houses, where people collaborate to finish the structures together.

I returned another day and met with local resident Patricio, who asked to be called Pinto. Pinto moved to the neighborhood thirty years ago from the southern rural community of San Ignacio, where, along with twelve brothers and sisters, he worked to produce corn, cotton, and other agricultural products on their small-scale farm. As an indication of the far reach of Stroessner's dynasty, Pinto explained that he has a brother who was disappeared under the dictatorship and has never been found. We walked with Pinto throughout the community, past small aqueducts, sewers, and bridges—all built by the neighbors. Gardens and livestock, parts of rural life, were everywhere, either among those families continuing farming traditions or who had recently arrived from the countryside.[36]

"Don," a pig farmer with one hundred pigs said, "This is a place that we made ourselves. We filled it up with dirt, rocks, and so on. It used to be all water. We've spent a lot of time and money to settle this. We have no help from the state. They only show up when they need votes, promise a lot and then disappear."[37] While the community activists say that they want more government support and involvement, the government's complete inattention to the community, in addition to police raids and demonizing media campaigns, have forced the community to create the change it wants to see by itself.

The community has demonstrated its capacity to organize itself on its own terms, without simply being utilized by politicians for votes. This capacity is the fruit of many years of organizing. "If people don't come to the meetings, we go to their houses," Pinto says. "When there's a big threat to the whole community we tape something on a cassette, rent speakers, put the speakers on a truck, and drive around to mobilize people, as well as with the community radio." This can happen to alert people about flooding or to convoke a protest or meeting. "Without community organizing nothing works. People would suffer more. Alone, you don't win anything, which is why the united social organizations are so important."

Throughout this panorama of social movement activity under the Lugo administration, there are notable differences between this terrain and that of other countries in South America examined here. On the one hand, Lugo is perhaps the leader farthest to the right and the least opposed to neoliberalism and the impunity of military criminals. The movements themselves are less energized, perhaps because of the nature of Paraguayan politics, the immense challenges posed by the soy industry, and the fact that the political and social recovery from the dictatorship is still beginning.

The contradictions of Lugo's administration, and the perceived need to support him in a defense against the established right-wing, also have demobilizing effects on the movements. The repressive nature of the state, military, and justice system, in collusion with police, military, and paramilitary groups, has had a devastating effect on movements. However, the dance in Paraguay is unresolved, as Lugo has not been in power for long. Particularly with the expansion of the soy industry, and the imminent threat of the right re-taking power from left-leaning leaders across the region, the situation in Paraguay merits close watching and consideration for anyone interested in working for social change in dire circumstances.

Republic Windows and Doors workers Melvin Maclin and Armando Robles (both in center), with fellow workers and supporters, celebrate in Chicago after winning the pay due to them following the closure of their factory. Photo by: Kari Lydersen

CHAPTER EIGHT

South America and the United States: Finding Common Ground in Crisis

Rain poured down in La Paz, Bolivia the day Barack Obama gave his inauguration speech. But the weather didn't stop thousands of Bolivians from marching in the streets in support of a new constitution, a document set to grant unprecedented rights to the country's indigenous majority. As chants and the explosions of Roman candles echoed throughout this capital city, Obama looked out from the television screen in a La Paz bar, offering words of wisdom that were somehow connected to many Bolivians' sense that democracy and good politics depended on a mobilized public taking to the streets.

"For as much as government can do and must do," Obama said, "it is ultimately the faith and determination of the American people upon which this nation relies."

Similarly, it has been the "faith and determination" of Bolivian social movements in their fight for a better world that paved the way to the election of indigenous President Evo Morales, and then pushed him to nationalize gas reserves, redistribute land to poor farmers, and enshrine long-overdue rights in a rewritten constitution.

The juxtaposition of Obama's orderly inauguration and the near-constant street mobilizations in La Paz raises the question: What can US activists facing economic crisis learn from South America's social movements? As unemployment skyrockets in the United States, and working for social change under an Obama administration remains challenging, US activists could apply the successful strategies of South American social movements to overcome economic crisis and destructive government policies.

In each case study in the previous chapters, I dissected the relationship between movements and governments. In some cases, after years of autonomous organizing, fiercely grassroots groups decided to run their own candidate. Elsewhere, movements avoided betrayal by not even engaging in electoral campaigns or backing the lesser of two evils in a presidential showdown. While some of the South American movements examined here sought autonomy from the government and remained in a protagonist role, others were coopted and undermined by party politics or the state. Operating in diverse circumstances, movements drew from a variety of tactics and strategies. The situation is similar in the US with the fluctuation of movements against war, globalization, or free trade, and these movements' relations with the government and electoral campaigns. Under the devastating and repressive policies of President George W. Bush, extended now with the "hope and change" rhetoric of Obama, we see such fluctuation in the activity of movements.

In engaging with this dance with the state, movements can effectively shift or transform policy in important areas, but only if they are strong. "Obama energized a great many people," writes Noam Chomsky. "If they fade away, or simply take instructions, we can expect little from his administration. If they become organized and active, and undertake to be independent voices in policy formation and implementation, a great deal can be achieved—as in the past, and elsewhere today, notably South America."[1]

In the cases outlined in this chapter, activists in the US drew inspiration from autonomous movements in South America. These movements include worker occupations and cooperatives in Argentina, the fight for access to water in Bolivia, and the landless struggle in Brazil. The corresponding examples in the US are the occupation of a factory in Chicago in 2008, struggles for access to water across the US, and the Take Back the Land group in Florida. Rather than actual movements, these are isolated actions and events by groups that reflect anger and tactics around the US. Still, the basic parallels with similar actions in the south show that South American movement strategies can be used internationally in the fight for social change.

Activating Democracy

The question of engaging the state and elections is as pressing among US activists as it has been for their counterparts in the south. In the US, many people believe that voting between a Democrat and Republican is the most important political act citizens can perform in

a democracy. Yet this energy that goes into the campaigns and elections of the lesser of two evils is misspent, as historian Howard Zinn
points out. "Would I support one candidate against another? Yes,
for two minutes—the amount of time it takes to pull the lever down
in the voting booth." Leading up to and following that act, Zinn
says, energy should be spent organizing, agitating, and educating for
a better society, building a movement to rattle the pillars of power.
"Voting is easy and marginally useful, but it is a poor substitute for
democracy, which requires direct action by concerned citizens."[2]
With a mobilized public, it matters less what president is in office,
as the president will have to answer to the power of the movements.

When Franklin Roosevelt was elected in 1932, he was far from
being a leftist. The most progressive of FDR's policies were the
results of grassroots pressure from below. According to a widely
cited legend, he once told labor constituents who were demanding
radical reforms, "I agree with you, I want to do it, now make me do
it." Howard Zinn notes of that relationship, "Where organized labor
was strong, Roosevelt moved to make some concessions to working
people."[3] Whether FDR had a heartfelt mission to help the working
class or was forced to do so against his will isn't the point. The point
is that little, if anything, ever happens on the state level without a
mobilized populace.

As Emma Goldman reminds us, extra-electoral organizing in the
US has yielded momentous results: "Universal suffrage itself owes
its existence to direct action. If not for the spirit of rebellion, of the
defiance on the part of the American revolutionary fathers, their pos-
terity would still wear the King's coat. If not for the direct action of a
John Brown and his comrades, America would still trade in the flesh
of the black man."[4]

While these uprisings led to historic institutional, cultural, and
policy changes, the movements for these rights and changes built
a better society through action. New forms of social relations can
indeed emerge among people in movements, people who build a
better world with their own hands rather than waiting for a savior
or president to deliver reforms from on high. Within that strategy,
Zinn said, it is important to "organize ourselves in such a way that
means correspond to the ends, and to organize ourselves in such a

way as to create the kind of human relationship that should exist in future society."[5] Once that model of human relationship and organization is developed within the movement, electoral victories become less relevant. We see examples of this with the MST in Brazil and the piqueteros and occupied factory movement in Argentina—among other South American movements.

Moving beyond traditional concepts of democracy and acting outside the logic of the state has been beneficial to movements throughout history. Working toward utopia within the autonomous territory of the movement means a new world can be created without the blessing of the state or capitalism, but according to the movement's logic and reality. "[B]y acting in a different world we actually bring forth that world," the Turbulence Collective writes. "Take the example of Rosa Parks who simply refused to move to the back of the bus. She wasn't making a demand, she wasn't even in opposition, she was simply acting in a different world."[6] In the US, as in South America, numerous groups are fighting for social change by applying such philosophies and approaches. The question is how to cross-pollinate these ideas and tactics even more, learning from both the victories and the mistakes of movements on both sides of the Rio Grande.

One international gathering that embodies the values of such cross-border organizing and solidarity is the annual World Social Forum which began in Brazil in 2001 to encourage collaboration and education between social movements from across the world. In 2004, I interviewed Michael Hardt, the co-author, with Antonio Negri, of *Multitude: War and Democracy in the Age of Empire*, about the role the World Social Forums and similar encounters can have in globalizing social justice. Hardt explained that at one of the meetings he attended at a WSF in Porto Alegre,

> [W]e had Italians, *piqueteros* from Argentina and a group from a movement in South Africa that is against these electricity and water cut offs in Durban and Johannesburg. It was great having three of them talk to each other, because even in a straightforward, tactical way they are experiencing the same thing, the same kinds of police repression and the same kinds of struggles. And it was not really learning from each other, but recognizing a kind of commonality

that then creates new relationships... It is that kind of thing that
has to happen on a much larger scale.

Developing the ties to learn from each other across borders is
essential. It is also important to consider the differences. The reaction to neoliberalism and its collapse has been, and will continue to
be, different in the north and south due to the diverse historical, economic, social, and cultural differences in each country. I don't mean
to suggest applying South American social movement tactics directly
to communities in the US. That would simply repeat the same mis-
take the International Monetary Fund consistently makes when it
blindly applies policies without considering the local culture, history,
and political reality of a given place.

And while I won't attempt to provide here, as I did with certain
countries in South America, an overview of the relationship between
social movements and the state in the US (that would be for another
book), it is important to consider certain relevant themes and currents in US politics and social movements that relate to the experiences in South America.

Chicago: Crisis and Action

The creativity displayed among the workers who occupied factories
and businesses in Argentina in the wake of that country's economic
crisis captured the imagination of the world. Those occupations and
worker-run models have proven to be viable, long-term alternatives to top-down capitalist work places. A clear connection between
social movement strategies in the north and south emerged in early
December 2008, when over 200 workers at Chicago's Republic
Windows and Doors factory were laid off and decided to fight back.
Gathering blankets, sleeping bags, and food, they occupied their
plant, demanding the severance and vacation pay owed to them. The
Republic workers began seeking ways to re-open their factory and
potentially operate it as a worker-run cooperative, further echoing
the movement in Argentina.

In Argentina in 2001, hundreds of worker cooperatives were
formed by workers after the occupations under the slogan "Occupy,

Resist, Produce." During the occupation of the factory in Chicago, workers and supporters chanted, "You got bailed out, we got sold out," referring to the fact that Bank of America—a lender to Republic—received $25 billion of a $700 billion government bail-out, only to cut off credit to Republic, contributing to the closure of the factory.

Leading up to the closure, workers caught wind of the boss's plans to lay them off: the owner was clandestinely trucking machinery from the Chicago plant to a factory set up in Iowa. Workers were given three days notice that they would be laid off without vacation and severance pay. After being dismissed from work, all the workers voted unanimously for occupation, a tactic they had been planning for weeks after finding out the machinery was being trucked out.

Mark Meinster, the international representative for United Electrical Workers, the union of the Republic workers, commented on the powerful feeling in the factory: "They had been working there for decades, and to be thrown out in the cold without a job right before Christmas, it was a slap in the face. We couldn't have gotten people out of there if we'd wanted to."[7] Desperate circumstances called for desperate measures, and pushed the workers together in solidarity, much like their counterparts in Argentina.

Workers were struck by the sharp inequalities forcing them out of a job and into a factory occupation. Republic worker Elisa Romo, forty-six, a single mother of four sons, one of whom joined his mom in support, said, "They give all this money to banks, but they won't help the regular people. We don't want anything that isn't ours, we just want what's owed to us."[8]

The solidarity the workers developed over the years together helped prepare them for the organizational tasks ahead of them. They began seeking allies in the labor, religious, and political sectors to support the occupation, and coordinated the food supplies and media relations. They decided that it would tactically make sense to target the Bank of America with their initial demands, as it was the institution that cut off the company's credit.[9]

Chicago-based journalist Kari Lydersen writes in *Revolt on Goose Island*, a book on the occupation,

As fires blazed out of several trash drums, workers and supporters formed a line to throw the bags of food hand to hand from the truck up the sidewalk through the crowd into the factory, a lively exercise accompanied by much chanting and cheering. The workers' moods were balanced on a precipice between elated at the attention and grim, given the harsh reality they could be facing.[10]

The workers' tactics, which pushed the boundaries of the law and challenged mainstream conceptions of legitimate responses to the economic crisis, proved useful in the end. After six days of occupation, Bank of America and other lenders relented, agreeing to pay the workers approximately $2 million in severance and vacation pay plus health insurance. But the workers didn't stop there; they began filing charges against their former employer for failing to give them sufficient notice of plans to shut the factory down.

The workers received support from people across the country in the form of solidarity rallies, monetary donations, blankets, and food. "That this support was on a scale unthinkable only a year ago is proof that this action spoke to the desire of working-class people to seek ways to resist the current economic onslaught," Meinster explained to me. However, for the action to take hold among workers in similar situations, "organized labor will have to take some measure of risk, embracing militant tactics when necessary and abandoning its reliance on political maneuvering as the primary means for the advancement of a working class agenda."

The strategies applied by these workers explicitly drew from Argentina. Meinster explained that in deciding on labor tactics, the Republic workers learned from examples of landless farmer occupations and worker cooperatives in South America, including those in Argentina. "We drew on the Argentine factory occupations to the extent that they show that during an economic crisis, workers' movements are afforded a wider array of tactical options," Meinster explained. "In fact, the film *The Take* [a documentary on worker occupations and cooperatives in Argentina] was screened in the factory during the occupation in a makeshift theatre set up in the locker room."

The workers participating in this action understood the terrain they were operating in, pressured officials to respond, and maintained their own autonomy as a work force by utilizing direct action and the solidarity that had grown between them as co-workers forced into a desperate situation. The similarities between the workers' actions in Chicago and Argentina show that labor strategies to fight economic crises can be applied as internationally as the free market policies that contributed to these problems in the first place.

Water Without Borders

While direct action worked in Chicago and Argentina, organizing around the right to a fundamental resource for survival—water—has proven to be a powerful tactic in the fight for social change around the world. A number of struggles against the privatization and high prices of water have been waged across the north and south. Many struggles in the US mirror those in South America, particularly in Cochabamba and El Alto, Bolivia and Buenos Aires, Argentina, where many of the same strategies to keep water in public hands were used. Similarly, the tactics employed by activists to fight for water rights and put this resource back into the public's hands have been similar across borders. One emblematic case in this global struggle is the story of Highland Park in Michigan.

Highland Park is a city located between Detroit and the suburbs, and is known as the birthplace of the assembly line. Thousands of people used to work in the Ford and Chrysler plants there. Chrysler closed up shop in the 1980s, taking the business elsewhere, and unemployment spiked. With a shrinking population and few jobs, there weren't any taxes to pay for city services and infrastructure, including the police and fire department. The city was going to go bankrupt, and the state called in private emergency financial planner Ramona Pearson to help.[11]

Pearson turned out to be a neoliberal zealot. Under her watch, the school, library, and garbage collection services were all shut down. She saw the city's municipal water system as a way to generate income for the city, and hoped to bleed money out of the impoverished residents by charging them exorbitant rates for water, a resource they couldn't do without. Pearson cut the water company's costs by firing most of its employees and then jacked up the water fees. When people couldn't pay the fees, their access was shut off. If residents didn't pay their back fees, Pearson's office connected the bills to people's property taxes, meaning that if they didn't pay their water bill, they would lose their home. The changes had far-reaching results. Many people were evicted from their homes and others had their children taken away from them by social services.[12]

Water, indeed, proved to be a vital service. And Pearson was willing to capitalize on that need. Yet Pearson and her consultants—all of whom were bringing in six figure salaries throughout this process—were not expecting a movement for water rising up out of Highland Park's desperation.[13] Similar to other water struggles in South America, this fight in Detroit sprang out of a lack of accountability among neoliberal leaders and their desire to put a need for funds above the need to address the human right to water.

Marian Kramer, co-chair of the National Welfare Rights Union said that in the period of 2001–2002, 40,700 people in her community had their water shut off because of inability to pay the bills.[14] "When a person doesn't have water, which is a prerequisite for survival, this is a violation of one's human rights. Neither agencies nor companies should be in complicity to punish the poor."[15] The irony was regularly driven home that though Highland Park was surrounded by the Great Lakes, the residents could not afford water.

As in Cochabamba, Bolivia just a few years earlier, citizens of Highland Park banded together against the bill increases and shut offs. Kramer explained, "We held direct-action campaigns against the Detroit Water and Sewage Department (DWSD) and finally developed a water affordability plan so no one would have to pay more than forty dollars [per month] and so there would be no water shutoffs." The activists pressured city council, exposing the fact that the public water system was being used as a tool to extract money from poor residents to keep the city government financially afloat, and was on the road to becoming privatized entirely.[16] The water rights group rallied support among local citizens to fight against the city's powerful consultants. The coalition fought, organized, and began to see the fruits of their labor when the governor banned water shutoffs in the winter.

After protests, radio shows, and outreach to defeat a plan to privatize the water system, the community was defiant at an emotional city council meeting. At the end of the heated meeting, a majority of the city council, responding to the citizens' concerns, voted against the privatization plan. After the battle, the governor asked Pearson and her consultants to resign; their salaries had cost the city over one million dollars.[17]

In February of 2007, thanks to citizens' pressure, the city council voted against a plan to increase water rates even more.[18] Marian Kramer said, "The fight in Highland Park is also the fight in Detroit. The fight in Highland Park is also the fight ... in Benton Harbor, in Flint, in Johannesburg, South Africa, in China, and the places where it comes to the question of water. It becomes a global problem."[19]

The fight for access to water is a clear connection between people's struggle across national and state lines. In 1998, the city of Atlanta signed a $428 million contract with United Water—a subsidiary of the major French consortium Suez, the same company that tried to privatize Buenos Aires' water around the same period. The contract was due to last for 20 years. At the time, United Water had the largest contract for water privatization in the US.[20] The move came when companies around the world were trying to profit off what had largely been a public-run service. Privatizing water had become a hallmark of neoliberalism. It was a money-making scheme that profited off of a fundamental resource. "This is a market with a huge potential," said Michael Chesser, United Water's chairman and chief executive, about the opportunity he saw in Atlanta.[21]

The management issues that arose in Atlanta are typical of the problems associated with privatization around the world. United Water conducted their operations in a corrupt manner, forging documents to over-bill the city for repairs. The company also fired over half of the employees in the water service to cut costs, and then went ahead and raised the water rates for consumers, including a 12 percent increase each year for sewer rates.[22] The quality of the water management also went down under private control; a number of "boil-water alerts" were issued for health safety concerns and fire hydrants were left in disrepair.[23]

The city terminated the contract in 2003, after massive outcries over the private company's poor service and rate increases. "Water is the worst thing to privatize," Clair Muller, chair of the City Council's utility committee in Atlanta, said. "It's what we need to live. I think that's key to the whole debate—are we going to lose control over functions that are essential to life?"[24]

Like movements around South America fighting for access to basic resources and services, it comes down to an issue of control and profit. Should corporations profit off of the need for water? Should governments be allowed to mismanage this resource in the name of neoliberalism? When people in the north and south organized to defend their own human rights against the state or a corporation, they wielded a power that overcame financial authority and political clout. That is the crux of the question for many of the challenges facing people and movements around the world—to organize within the framework of the law and the state, or fight for what you need on your own terms. The latter tactic is what drives many movements in South America, and is what inspired the Take Back the Land movement in Florida.

Taking Back the Land

In a move that is very similar to the tactics and philosophy of Brazil's landless movement, in the afternoon on October 23, 2006, homeless people, activists, and local citizens took over—"liberated"—a vacant lot in Miami, Florida. For the following six months, approximately 150 people lived in this shantytown. The community was called Umoja Village after the Swahili word for unity.

Max Rameau, the leader of the occupation, was born in Haiti. His father was a doctor and his mother a nurse. He moved to the US at a young age, but lived in Haiti during the summers. Understanding the disparities of wealth in Haiti led him to his housing activism.

In 2001, Miami-Dade County officials leveled a sixty-two-unit, low-income apartment building, putting hundreds of people into the streets without homes. Nothing was ever rebuilt in its place. In 2006, Rameau and others, largely homeless people, took over the lot where the building had been and built a shantytown out of plywood and pallets.[25]

Before they took over the land, Rameau and his fellow activists scouted the city out for the right spot, planned the action well in advance with a legal team in place and the building supplies ready. They sought a broad coalition of support from other anti-gentri-fication groups in the area, and gathered food and supplies. They were careful, while garnering their support, to not let on where the occupation was actually going to take place in order to maintain the element of surprise. After taking over the land, new residents arrived to the village daily, as did supporters, journalists, and people who were simply curious.[26] The tactics and approach echoed those of the MST in Brazil in more ways than one.

The Umoja Village included some twenty small structures built from wood, a large kitchen area, two porta-potties, and a raised-water container functioning as a shower. The village was managed by its occupants, who came to decisions through discussion and vot-ing.[27] Rameau recounts how homeless people lived and organized their new home at Umoja:

> They voted on the rules of the community in which they lived and partook in its development and maintenance, cooking, cleaning, building shanties, a shower, a library and a welcome center. Some used the physical safety and food security to gather their thoughts and save money before moving up and on to an apartment or other living arrangements. Several residents became clean, returned to school or found employment, while living on the land.[28]

For many of the people there, it was the first time they had autonomy over their own lives, and exercised that control through the communal space and meetings of the village. "That was the real thing that happened there, people were given some real level of dignity," Rameau explained.[29] This philosophy of self management was reflected in one of the stated political goals of the Take Back the Land movement, which notes the need to not recreate, within the movement, the same hierarchy and power structures that gener-ally dominate the larger society: "[W]e build a new society in which people relate to one another differently and the power to make deci-sions about the Village is centered on them, not the politicians."[30] Such an objective was similar to Brazil's landless movement, which operates according to its own needs, building a new world within the settlement without bowing down to political leaders or parties.

Six months after this radical experiment in community activism began, the village burned down under suspicious circumstances. Following the fire, when banks began foreclosing on homes across the Miami area, Rameau took his activism elsewhere. In January of 2008, there were 4,574 homeless people in Miami-Dade County, and 4,725 foreclosed homes. "It's morally indefensible to have vacant homes sitting there, potentially for years, while you have human beings on the street," Rameau said.[31]

The solution was evident to Rameau; he worked to place homeless people in foreclosed homes. To find a place to squat, he checked foreclosure listings then looked at the houses to see what kind of shape they were in. Rameau said they screened people for drug addiction and mental illness before setting them up with a home, made sure they could do their own repairs on the house, and pay the water, heating, and electric bills.[32]

The first homeless people to enter into a home with Rameau's help were Cassandra and Jason, parents in their late twenties with two young kids. Before occupying the house they had been living out of a van. When they moved in, a neighbor offered them electricity through an extension cord from his home.[33] Often, matching homeless people with a home meant they had a chance to get back on their feet, reorganize their lives, and move on.

In November of 2008, Rameau drove Marie Nadine Pierre and her 18 month old daughter to a new home. Pierre and her daughter had been homeless for a year. "My heart is heavy. I've lived in a lot of different shelters, a lot of bad situations," Pierre said. "In my own home, I'm free. I'm a human being now." She knew that she could be arrested for trespassing, breaking and entering, or vandalism, but also knew she could count on free legal defense from Rameau's network of supporters.[34]

In the context of the housing crisis, Rameau sees a "disconnect between the need and the law," and believes it is "immoral" to have people homeless in the streets when there are empty homes.[35] The MST in Brazil operates with a similar faith in direct action; by moving outside the scope of the law and acting illegally for a greater cause, they successfully force authorities to recognize the legitimacy of their actions and needs. In many cases, it is a simple question of priorities, and whether the government and justice systems believe their duty is to uphold the rights of corporations and the wealthy over the rights of working, homeless, or landless people.

"Take Back the Land asserts that the right of human beings to housing supersedes the corporate drive to maximize profits," Rameau writes. "We advance that assertion by directly challenging existing laws which favor corporate profits over human needs."[36] Many South American movements—and some in the US—adhere to this belief in human needs trumping profit and the law, making them powerful forces for social change.

An Unwritten Future

Neoliberalism knows no borders; the poor majority is not immune to this economic model's wrath, regardless of nationality. It has devastated the working class, displaced communities, enslaved workers, and taken access to public services and resources out of the hands of the people who need them the most.

The challenges for movements are similar in the north and south. The same type of economic ideology seeks undermine workers rights from Buenos Aires to Chicago. The same water company, Suez, sought to privatize water in Bolivia and Atlanta. The same emphasis on corporate profit over human needs displaces people from Brazil to Miami. The same connections can be made among the strategies grassroots groups use to fight against these challenges. South American movements have been grappling with the horrors of neoliberalism for decades, so it makes sense that US activists might consider successful tactics and strategies from the south.

Applying South American movement strategies in the US is a clear reversal of an historic trend. The extraction of resources from the south to the north has empowered the US economy for over a century. US foreign policy toward South America has been dominated by the objective of protecting and expanding the US business presence in the region. Washington has supported coups and propped up dictators across the hemisphere for decades, most recently in Honduras. Too often, US diplomats, military officials, and international lenders have flown down to the south to apply harmful structural adjustments, teach torture techniques, fight against self-determination, and push for neoliberal economic policies. This destructive flow of knowledge from the north to the south has been devastating for working people across the continent. Instead, revolutionary tactics should be exported from the south to the north, reversing this general flow of knowledge, and replacing repressive strategies with those aimed at liberation.

The dance in South America examined in this book is instructive regarding the question of tying movement horses to electoral or state carts. The lessons learned from South America of cooptation, demobilization, opportunism, and repression are all applicable in the US.

The similarities between people of different nations and societies are often stronger than the differences. The structures of power that centralize wealth and exploit people and the environment all benefit from a division and disconnect between people across the world. When connections are made across borders to identify both the systems of oppression and the strategies to overcome them, a better world will indeed be possible. Central to the development of such connections is an analysis of the relationship between social movements and states. How movements dance with political parties, aspiring and incumbent presidents, and the government itself will decide the future of the planet.

Acknowledgments

While researching and writing this book, I benefited from the help and guidance of many wonderful friends across North and South America. They were there when the tear gas at street barricades turned into the confetti of presidential campaigns, and then back to tear gas again. Without their camaraderie, this book would never have been written.

A number of people helped me navigate the complicated terrain of the dance between social movements and states in various countries. Their analysis, knowledge and experience helped light the way on the journey of writing this book. Thanks to Carlos Arce, Pedro Caballero, Marco Castillo, Orlando Castillo, Marielle Cauthin, Patricia Costas, Leticia Galeano, Luis Gonzalez, Julio Mamani, Pablo Mamani, Julieta Ojeda Marguay and Mujeres Creando, Mark Mienster, Lucas Palero, Gilda Roa, Javiera Rulli, Oscar Vega and many more.

Thanks to my friend the late Bolivian hip-hop artist, activist, and teacher, Abraham Bojorquez. The actions and impact of his all-too-short life are a testament to how much good one person can do by practicing what they rap.

To fellow activists and affinity groups at Bard College from 1999 through the start of the Iraq War, your spirit, anger, and joy is present in these pages.

Thanks to everyone at AK Press, again, for believing in this book and seeing it through to the copy in your hands. As a collectively-run book publisher, they continue to do the impossible. Charles Weigl, the editor at AK for this book, proved that two heads are indeed better than one. His thoughtful and informed analysis strengthened this book considerably.

Thanks to Robin Lloyd and everyone at *Toward Freedom* for their support and community, and to Cyril Mychalejko, April Howard, and Jason Wallach at *Upside Down World*. This book reflects our years of writing and editing about Latin America together. Thanks to Sandy Baird and the students of Burlington College for many lively classroom discussions on South American politics.

I am grateful for all the journalists and media makers who apply a belief in solidarity and mutual aid to their everyday work. Michael Fox was a great comrade through every phase of the writing of this book, generously sharing his expertise, editing skills, and recommendations. Crucial input on key chapters was provided by Marie Trigona and Cyril Mychalejko. The insightful writing of Raúl Zibechi helped me see South America with new eyes, and served as a great resource for researching many of the countries discussed here.

Thanks to photographers Bear Guerra, Patricio Realpe, Sílvia Leindecker, Michael Fox, Joshua Lambert, Marie Trigona, and Kari Lydersen for their contributions. For translation and transcription help, thanks to David Brookbank, Ruxandra Guidi, Maria Hoisington, and Maggie von Vogt.

To my friends in Burlington, Vermont, Carl, Jess, Graham, Sara, Sam, Molly, Joe, S'ra, Jonny, Jen, and many more, thank you for making this city a home away from home.

My family has always aided and abetted me, and this book project is no exception. My political orientation has a lot to do with my parents. Suzanne Summers, my mother, brought me to food cooperative meetings when I was a kid, and I attended Wobbly (Industrial Workers of the World) union meetings down the road from our rural house with my father, Jon Dangl. The co-op was a great place to score delicious slices of cheese, and the Wobbly meetings were full of exciting stories of epic struggles against corrupt bosses. More than that, however, these experiences helped instill in me a tendency toward collective processes and anti-authoritarian politics. Thank you!

Thanks to my grandparents, Doc and Betty Summers. My grandfather, an active participant in the 1960s civil rights movement, and my grandmother, whose house as a child was a helpful stopping off point for hoboes seeking food during the Great Depression, both taught me about justice and compassion through their example. Thanks to my brothers, Nick and Jimmy Dangl, for their support, humor and inspiration.

Finally, just as I would like to thank sunlight and the person who invented coffee, I would like to thank April Howard, my partner of nearly a decade. We have traveled the globe together and shared everything. Please accept this book as you might a bouquet of flowers: it is a demonstration of gratitude and love, and a product of our life together.

While I received insightful advice from many of the people listed here, I did not apply all of their suggestions, and so I take full responsibility for any shortcomings or mistakes present in this book.

Notes

Introduction

1   Author interview with Pedro Caballero, April 2009.

2   Author interview with Ramón Denis, April 2009.

3   John Steinbeck, *The Grapes of Wrath*, Penguin Classics, (New York: Viking Press, 1939).

4   *The Unedited Diaries of Carolina Maria de Jesus*, (Piscataway: Rutgers University Press, December 1, 1998).

5   Herbert S. Klein, *A Concise History of Bolivia*, (Cambridge: Cambridge University Press, 2003), 212.

6   Vijay Prashad, *The Darker Nations: A People's History of the Third World*, (New York: New Press, 2007), 135–136.

7   Quoted in June Nash, *We Eat the Mines and the Mines Eat Us: Dependency and Exploitation in Bolivian Tin Mines*, (New York: Columbia University Press, 1993), 274–275.

8   Emma Goldman, "The Individual, Society and the State," (1940), http://dwardmac.pitzer.edu/anarchist_archives/goldman/goldmanindiv.html.

9   Noam Chomsky, *Chomsky on Anarchism*, (Oakland: AK Press, 2005), 121.

10 John Holloway, *Change the World Without Taking Power: The Meaning of Revolution Today*, (London: Pluto Press, 2002), 12–15.

11 Rebecca Solnit, *A Paradise Built in Hell: The Extraordinary Communities that Arise in Disaster*, (New York: Viking, 2009), 90–91.

12 Atilio Borón, "Latin American Social Movements: Standing up to Friends," *NACLA Report on the Americas*, (February 27, 2008), http://news.nacla.org/2008/02/27/latin-american-social-movements-standing-up-to-friends/.

13 Raúl Zibechi, *Territorios en Resistencia: Cartografía política de las periferias urbanas latinoamericanas*, (Buenos Aires: Lavaca editora, 2008), 132–136, 149.

14 Noam Chomsky, "Answers by Noam Chomsky," *ZNet*, http://www.zmag.org/chomsky_repliesana.htm.

15 Quoted in Michael McCaughan, *True Crime: Rodolfo Walsh and the Role of the Intellectual in Latin American Politics*, (London: Latin America Bureau, 2002).

16 Benjamin Kohl and Linda Farthing, *Impasse in Bolivia: Neoliberal Hegemony and Popular Resistance*, (New York: Zed Books, 2006), 15–18. For more information see Robin Hahnel, *The ABCs of Political Economy*, (London: Pluto Press, 2002);

Douglas Dowd, *Capitalism and Its Economics*, (London: Pluto Press, 2004), and Noam Chomsky, *Profit Over People*, (New York: Seven Stories Press, 1998), and *Radical Priorities*, (Oakland: AK Press, 2003).

17   Larry Rohter, "Bush Faces Tough Time in South America," *The New York Times*, (November 2, 2005), http://www.nytimes.com/2005/11/02/international/americas/02latin.html?_r=1.

18   Benjamin Dangl, "Is George Bush Restarting Latin America's 'Dirty Wars'?" *Alternet*, (August 31, 2007), http://www.alternet.org/world/58605/.

19   For more information see Benjamin Dangl, "U.S. Bases in Colombia Rattle the Region," *The Progressive* (March 2010), http://progressive.org/danglmarch10.html; Benjamin Dangl, "Showdown in Honduras: The Rise and Uncertain Future of the Coup," *Toward Freedom*, (June 29, 2009), http://towardfreedom.com/home/content/view/1615/54/; Benjamin Dangl, "The Road to Zelaya's Return: Money, Guns and Social Movements in Honduras," *Toward Freedom*, (September 21, 2009), http://towardfreedom.com/home/content/view/1687/54/; Benjamin Dangl, "Profiting From Haiti's Crisis," *Toward Freedom*, (January 18, 2010), http://towardfreedom.com/home/content/view/1827/54/. Benjamin Dangl, "Latin America Breaks Free," *The Progressive*, (February 2009), http://www.pro-gressive.org/mag/dangl0209.html.

20   Eduardo Galeano, "Window on Utopia," in *Walking Words* (New York: W.W. Norton, 1995); reprinted in *The Nation* (June 12, 1995).

Chapter One

1   June Nash, *We Eat the Mines and the Mines Eat Us: Dependency and Exploitation in Bolivian Tin Mines*, (New York: Columbia University Press, 1993), 146.

2   Author interview with Claudia Yucra, March 2009.

3   Quoted in Benjamin Dangl, "New Politics in Old Bolivia: Public Opinion and Evo Morales," *Upside Down World*, (November 28, 2007), http://upsidedownworld.org/main/bolivia-archives-31/1021-new-politics-in-old-bolivia-public-opinion-and-evo-morales.

4   For an overview of recent Bolivian social movement and political history see *The Price of Fire: Resource Wars and Social Movements in Bolivia* (Oakland: AK Press, 2007).

5   For more information on the US war on drugs in Bolivia, see the Andean Information Network, http://ain-bolivia.org/.

6   Benjamin Dangl, "Land as a Center of Power in Bolivia," *Toward Freedom*,

(December 7, 2006), http://towardfreedom.com/home/content/view/938/.

7   Author interview with Gustavo Torrico, March 2009.

8   Author interview with Oscar Vega, January 2009.

9   Luis Tapia, *The New Latin American Left: Utopia Reborn*, (London: Pluto Press, 2008), 226–229.

10   Author interview with Julieta Ojeda Marguay, February 2009.

11   Quoted in Raúl Zibechi, *Territorios en Resistencia: Cartografía política de las periferias urbanas latinoamericanas*, (Buenos Aires: Lavaca editora, 2008), 135.

12   Ibid., 109.

13   Author interview with Patricia Costas, March 2009.

14   See Benjamin Dangl, "The Machine Gun and The Meeting Table: Bolivian Crisis in a New South America," *Toward Freedom*, (September 16, 2008), http://towardfreedom.com/home/content/view/1408/1/.

15   Quoted in Raúl Zibechi, "Plan 3000: Resistance and Social Change at the Heart of Racism," *Americas Program*, (May 18, 2010), http://www.cipamericas.org/archives/1714.

16   Quoted in Clifton Ross, "Bolivia in Dialogue: Between Hope and Civil War," *Upside Down World*, (October 1, 2008), http://upsidedownworld.org/main/bolivia-archives-31/1507-bolivia-in-dialogue-between-hope-and-civil-war.

17   Franz Chávez, "Bolivia: Morales Leads March for New Constitution," *IPS News*, (October 13, 2008), http://ipsnews.net/news.asp?idnews=44249.

18   Eduardo Avila, "Bolivia: Pro-Government March Arrives to La Paz," *Global Voices Online*, (October 21, 2008), http://globalvoicesonline.org/2008/10/21/bolivia-pro-government-march-arrives-to-la-paz/.

19   Author interview with Pablo Mamani, March 2009.

20   Author interview with Ismael Herrera Lovera, March 2009.

21   Author interview with Julio Mamani, March 2009.

22   Quoted in Benjamin Kohl and Linda Farthing, *Impasse in Bolivia: Neoliberal Hegemony and Popular Resistance*, (New York: Zed Books, 2006), 40–41.

23   Author interview with Carlos Arce, March 2009.

24   For information and analysis on regional and local elections in April 2010, see Emily Achtenberg, "Bolivia: Elections Deepen Local Democracy," *NACLA Report on the Americas*, (May 21, 2010), https://nacla.org/node/6579.

Chapter Two

1   Quoted in Suzana Sawyer, *Crude Chronicles: Indigenous Politics, Multinational Oil,*

and Neoliberalism in Ecuador, (Durham: Duke University Press, 2004), 149–151.

2   Quoted in Ibid.

3   Quoted in Ibid, 187–188.

4   David Dudenhoefer, "For Ecuador's indigenous nations: A new constitution and familiar problems," *Indian Country Today*, (August 28, 2009), http://www.indian countrytoday.com/archive/53944647.html.

5   Al Gedicks, *Resource Rebels: Native Challenges to Mining and Oil Corporations*, (Boston: South End Press, 2001), 67–68.

6   Ibid.

7   Quoted in Nikolas Kozloff, *Revolution!: South America and the Rise of the New Left*, (New York: Palgrave Macmillan, 2009), 25–29,

8   Ibid., 27–28.

9   Nic Paget-Clarke, "Interview with Dr. Luis Macas of CONAIE," *In Motion Magazine*, (August 31, 2007), http://inmotionmagazine.com/global/lm_int_eng.html.

10   James Petras and Henry Veltmeyer, *Social Movements and State Power: Argentina, Brazil, Bolivia, Ecuador*, (London: Pluto Press, 2005), 160–161.

11   Marc Becker "Ecuador, Indigenous Uprisings," in *Oxford Encyclopedia of the Modern World*, Ed. Peter N. Stearns, (2008 e-reference edition), (Oxford: Oxford University Press, 2008).

12   Minorities at Risk Project, "Chronology for Indigenous Highland Peoples in Ecuador," United Nations, (2004), http://www.unhcr.org/refworld/docid/469f38831e.html.

13   Allen Gerlach, *Indians, Oil, and Politics: A Recent History of Ecuador*, (Wilmington: Scholarly Resources Books, 2003), 69–71.

14   Ibid., 72.

15   CONAIE, "CONAIE: A Brief History," *Native Web*, (December 1992), http://conaie.nativeweb.org/conaie1.html.

16   Scott H. Beck and Kenneth J. Mijeski, "Barricades and Ballots: Ecuador's Indians and The Pachakutik Political Movement," *Ecuadorian Studies*, (September 2001), http://www.yachana.org/ecuatorianistas/journal/1/beck.pdf.

17   Petras and Veltmeyer, *Social Movements and State Power*,147–149.

18   Sawyer, *Crude Chronicles*, 27–29, 41, 50–54.

19   Beck and Mijeski, "Barricades and Ballots." And Mark Becker 1996. "President of CONAIE runs for Congress.," *NACLA Report on the Americas*.

20   Gerlach, *Indians, Oil, and Politics*, 76–77.

21   James Petras, "Rebellion in Ecuador," *Z Magazine*, (April 2000), http://beta.zcommunications.org/rebellion-in-ecuador-by-james-petras.

22 Petras and Veltmeyer, *Social Movements and State Power*,149–151.

23 Ibid., 149–151, 155–159.

24 Rune Geertsen, "Interview with Luis Macas: 'We want a total transformation,'" *Upside Down World*, (September 19, 2006), http://upsidedownworld.org/main/content/view/433/1/.

25 Patricio Zhingri T., "Interview with Marlon Santi: New President of Ecuador's Indigenous Confederation," *Upside Down World*, (January 15, 2008), http://upsidedownworld.org/main/ecuador-archives-49/1087-interview-with-marlon-santi-new-president-of-ecuadors-indigenous-confederation.

26 Kees Biekart, "Seven theses on Latin American social movements and political change," *Transnational Institute*, (October 2005), http://www.tni.org//archives/archives_biekart_lamovements.

27 Juan Forero, "Ecuador's Leader Flees and Vice-president Replaces Him," *New York Times*, (April 21, 2005), http://www.nytimes.com/2005/04/21/international/americas/21ecuador.html?_r=1.

28 Geertsen, "Interview with Luis Macas."

29 Ibid.

30 Quoted in Cyril Mychalejko, "Ecuador on the Edge: A Tale of Two Presidential Candidates," *Toward Freedom*, (November 2, 2006), http://towardfreedom.com/home/content/view/914/.

31 Daniel Denvir, "Wayward Allies: President Rafael Correa and the Ecuadorian Left," *Upside Down World*, (July 25, 2008), http://upsidedownworld.org/main/ecuador-archives-49/1396-wayward-allies-president-rafael-correa-and-the-ecuadorian-left.

32 Mario Unda, *Movimientos Sociales: Nuevas Realidades, Nuevos Desafios*, (Buenos Aires: Observatorio Social de América Latina, 2006), 111.

33 Mark Engler, *How to Rule the World: The Coming Battle Over the Global Economy* (New York: Nation Books, 2008), 268.

34 Daniel Denvir, "Ecuador Defaults on Foreign Debt," *Upside Down World*, (December 11, 2008), http://upsidedownworld.org/main/content/view/1627/49/.

35 Nic Paget-Clarke, "Interview with Dr. Luis Macas of CONAIE," *In Motion Magazine*, (August 31, 2007), http://inmotionmagazine.com/global/lm_int_eng.html.

36 Ana María Larrea, *Movimientos Sociales: Nuevas Realidades, Nuevos Desafios*, (Buenos Aires: Observatorio Social de América Latina, 2006), 259–261.

37 Denvir, "Wayward Allies."

38 Dudenhoefer, "For Ecuador's indigenous nations."

39 Quoted in Paul Dosh and Nicole Kligerman, "Correa vs. Social Movements:

Showdown in Ecuador," *NACLA Report on the Americas*, (September 17, 2009), https://nacla.org/node/6124; and Naomi Klein, "Open Letter to President Rafael Correa Regarding Closure of Acción Ecológica," March 12, 2009.

40   Quoted in Jennifer Moore, "Swinging from the Right: Correa and Social Movements in Ecuador," *Upside Down World*, (May 12, 2009), http://upsidedownworld.org/main/ecuador-archives-49/1856-swinging-from-the-right-correa-and-social-movements-in-ecuador-.

41   Daniel Denvir, "Whither Ecuador? An Interview with Indigenous Activist and Politician Monica Chuji," *Upside Down World*, (November 6, 2008), http://upsidedownworld.org/main/ecuador-archives-49/1563-whither-ecuador-an-interview-with-indigenous-activist-and-politician-monica-chuji.

42   Denvir, "Wayward Allies."

43   Quoted in Ibid.

44   Quoted in Daniel Denvir and Thea Riofrancos, "CONAIE Indigenous Movement Condemns President Correa," *Latin America in Movement*, (May 16, 2008), http://alainet.org/active/24062&lang=es.

45   Dosh and Kligerman, "Correa vs. Social Movements."

46   Jennifer Moore, "Ecuadorians Protest New Water Law," *Upside Down World*, (September 29, 2009), http://upsidedownworld.org/main/content/view/2136/49/.

47   Quoted in Ahni, "Ecuador's Indigenous Movement Mobilizes for the Water," *Intercontinental Cry*, (September 28, 2009), http://intercontinentalcry.org/ecuador-indigenous-movement-mobilizes-for-water/.

48   Quoted in Daniel Denvir, "Mass Indigenous Protest In Defense of Water Caps Week of Mobilizations in Ecuador," *Upside Down World*, (November 20, 2008), http://upsidedownworld.org/main/content/view/1591/49/.

49   Gonzalo Ortiz, "Ecuador: Native Standoff Over Water Bill on Hold," *IPS News*, (May 19, 2010), http://ipsnews.net/news.asp?idnews=51504.

50   Marc Becker, "Ecuador: Left Turn?" *Against the Current*, (October 2009), http://www.solidarity-us.org/atc. In April of 2010, Correa helped approve a deal to allow the oil in Yasuni park to stay in the ground in an effort to protect the region's environment: "Ecuadorian President Confirms Deal to Leave Oil Under Yasuni Park," *Environmental News Service*, (April 26, 2010), http://www.ens-newswire.com/ens/apr2010/2010-04-26-02.html.

51   Tito Puenchir, "Two killed during protests against water laws in Ecuador," *Colonos*, (September 30, 2009), http://colonos.wordpress.com/2009/10/01/two-killed-during-protests-against-water-laws-in-ecuador/.

Chapter Three

1   Quoted in Marina Sitrin, *Horizontalism: Voices of Popular Power in Argentina*, (Oakland: AK Press, 2006), 32.

2   Raúl Zibechi, *Genealogía de la Revuelta*, (Montevideo: Nordan-Comunidad, 2003), 186–187.

3   "Scilingo admitió que hubo unos 200 'vuelos de la muerte,'" *InfoBae.com*, (January 20, 2005), http://www.infobae.com/notas/nota.php?Idx=163204&IdxSeccion=100558.

4   Duncan Green, *Silent Revolution: The Rise and Crisis of Market Economics in Latin America*, (New York: Monthly Review Press, 2003), 14–15. Also see Mark Weisbrot, "Argentina's Crisis, IMF's Fingerprints," *Washington Post*, (December 25, 2001), http://www.cepr.net/index.php/op-eds-&-columns/op-eds-&-columns/argentinas-crisis-imfs-fingerprints/.

5   Joseph E. Stiglitz, *Globalization and its Discontents* (New York: W. W. Norton & Company, 2003), 69.

6   Eric Toussaint, *Your Money or Your Life* (Chicago: Haymarket Books, 2005), 313–323.

7   Daniel Cieza, *Empire and Dissent: The United States and Latin America* (Durham: Duke University Press, 2008), 196–197.

8   Ibid., 196.

9   Patricia Alba, "Movimientos sociales: Entre la autonomía y la cooptación," *La Fogata*, http://www.lafogata.org/06arg/arg12/arg_15-4.htm.

10   "Picket and Pot Banger Together—Class recomposition in Argentina?," *Libcom. org*, (July 4, 2005), http://libcom.org/library/argentina-aufheben-11.

11   "The events that triggered Argentina's crisis," *BBC News*, (December 21, 2001), http://news.bbc.co.uk/2/hi/business/1721103.stm.

12   Green, *Silent Revolution*, 13, 14–15.

13   "New man takes helm in Argentina," *BBC News*, (January 2, 2002), http://news.bbc.co.uk/2/hi/americas/1737562.stm.

14   Mark Engler, *How to Rule the World: The Coming Battle Over the Global Economy* (New York: Nation Books, 2008), 261.

15   Jim Straub, "Argentina's Piqueteros and Us," *TomDispatch*, (March 2, 2004), http://www.tomdispatch.com/post/1287/the_argentine_model.

16   Quoted in Lavaca Collective, *Sin Patrón: Stories from Argentina's Worker-Run Factories*, (Chicago: Haymarket Books, 2007), 113–114.

17   Andrés Gaudin, "Occupying, Resisting, Producing: Argentine Workers Take Over Abandoned Factories," *Dollars and Sense*, (March/April 2004), http://

www.thirdworldtraveler.com/South_America/Occupy_Resist_Argentina.html.

18   Quoted in Ibid.

19   Quoted in Lavaca Collective, *Sin Patrón*, 133–134.

20   Quoted in Ibid.,133–134.

21   Quoted in Ibid., 134–135, 138–140).

22   Ben Dangl, "Cerámica de Cuyo: A Profile of Worker Control in Argentina," *Toward Freedom*, (June 20, 2007), http://towardfreedom.com/home/content/view/1061/54/.

23   Rafael Azul, "Argentina's police killings raise specter of dictatorship," *World Socialist Website*, (July 2, 2002), http://www.wsws.org/articles/2002/jul2002/arg-j02.shtml.

24   Ojo Obrero, "Piqueteros Carajo!" (2002), http://www.ojoobrero.org/peliculas/piqueteros_carajo.html.

25   Ezequiel Adamovsky, "Who is Nestor Kirchner, Argentina's New President?," *ZNet*, (May 20, 2003), http://beta.zcommunications.org/who-is-n-stor-kirchner-argentina-s-new-president-by-ezequiel-adamovsky.

26   Quoted in Sitrin, *Horizontalism*, 123.

27   Zibechi, *Genealogía de la Revuelta*, 206.

28   Quoted in Andres Lopez, Tim Jack, & Marie Trigona, "Argentina's Elections," *Z Magazine*, (July/August 2003), http://www.thirdworldtraveler.com/South_America/Argentina%27s_Elections.html.

29   Mark Engler, *How to Rule the World*, 262–263.

30   Tariq Ali, *Pirates of the Caribbean: Axis of Hope* (New York: Verso, 2006), 40.

31   Cieza, *Empire and Dissent*, 199.

32   Steven Levitsky and María Victoria Murillo, "Argentina: From Kirchner to Kirchner," *Journal of Democracy*, (April 2008), http://www.columbia.edu/~mm2140/Publications%20in%20English_files/JOD08.pdf.

33   Quoted in "Dirty War generals' portraits removed," *Los Angeles Times*, (March 25, 2004), http://articles.sfgate.com/2004-03-25/news/17416658_1_military-rule-dedication-ceremony-governors-from-kirchner-s-peronist.

34   Hector Tobar, "Argentine Court Voids Amnesty in 'Dirty War,'" *Los Angeles Times*, (June 15, 2005), http://articles.latimes.com/2005/jun/15/world/fg-argen15.

35   Andrés Gaudin, *Dispatches from Latin America: On the Frontlines Against Neoliberalism*, (Boston: South End Press, 2006), 78.

36   Quoted in Geraldine Lievesley and Steve Ludlam, *Reclaiming Latin America: Experiments in Radical Social Democracy*, (Zed Books, 2009), 211–214.

37   Quoted in Ibid.

38   Quoted in Moira Birss, "The Piquetero Movement: Organizing for Democracy and Social Change in Argentina's Informal Sector," *The Journal of the International Institute*, (Winter 2005), http://quod.lib.umich.edu/cgi/t/text/text-idx?c=j ii;view=text;rgn=main;idno=4750978.0012.206.

39   Quoted in Gaudin, *Dispatches from Latin America*, 83.

40   James Petras, "Latin America: Social Movements in Times of Economic Crises," *Axis of Logic*, (August 13, 2009), http://axisoflogic.com/artman/publish/Article_56635.shtml.

41   Also see H.I.J.O.S. website: http://www.hijos-capital.org.ar/index.php?option=com_content&view=article&id=20&Itemid=399

42   Petras, "Latin America."

43   Cieza, *Empire and Dissent*, 200–202.

44   Jim Straub, "Argentina's Piqueteros and Us," *TomDispatch*, (March 2, 2004), http://www.tomdispatch.com/post/1287/the_argentine_model.

45   Gabriel Espinosa Gonzalez and Matthew B. Riley, "Argentina's President Kirchner Continues His Daring Departure from Past Practices," *Council on Hemispheric Affairs*, (October 20, 2004), http://www.coha.org/argentina%E2%80%99s-president kirchner-continues-his-daring-departure-from past-practices/.

46   Gaudin, *Dispatches from Latin America*, 79

47   Federico Schuster, *The New Latin American Left: Utopia Reborn*, (Pluto Press, 2008), 176–177.

48   Ibid., 178.

49   Gaudin, *Dispatches from Latin America*, 79–81.

50   Quoted in Sitrin, *Horizontalism*, 125.

Chapter Four

1   "Tortas fritas y música, en otra fiesta del Frente Amplio," *La Nacion*, (March 2, 2010) http://www.lanacion.com.ar/nota.asp?nota_id=1238905.

2   Quoted in "Galeano: 'Es el presidente que más se parece a lo que somos,'" *Página/12*, (March 1, 2010), http://www.pagina12.com.ar/imprimir/diario/ultimas/subnotas/141211-45484-2010-03-01.html.

3   Quoted in Diana Cariboni, "Uruguay: New President Aims for Leap in Development," *IPS News*, (March 1, 2010), http://ipsnews.net/news.asp?idnews=50503.

4   Michael Fox, "Uruguay's Frente Amplio: From Revolution to Dilution," *Upside Down World*, (June 26, 2007), http://upsidedownworld.org/main/uruguay-archives-48/788-uruguays-frente-amplio-from-revolution-to-dilution.

5   Ibid.

6   Quoted in Ibid.

7   Quoted in Stella Calloni, "Elecciones en Uruguay: la cuestión nacional está en el centro," *Red Voltaire*, (October 23, 2004), http://www.voltairenet.org/article122498.html#auteur3643.

8   Geraldine Lievesley and Steve Ludlam, *Reclaiming Latin America: Experiments in Radical Social Democracy*, (Zed Books, 2009), 30.

9   Amnesty International, "Uruguay must annul law that protects police and military torture suspects," *Amnesty International*, (October 20, 2009), http://www.amnesty.org/en/news-and-updates/news/uruguay-must-annul-law-protects-police-and-military-torture-suspects-20091020.

10 Raúl Zibechi, "The Uruguayan Left and the Construction of Hegemony," *Dispatches from Latin America: On the Frontlines Against Neoliberalism*, (Boston: South End Press, 2008), 135–136.

11 Ibid., 135–136.

12 David Butler and Austin Ranney, *Referendums Around the World: The Growing Use of Direct Democracy*, (Washington DC: AEI Press, 1994), 7.

13 Quoted in Marcela Valente, "Latin America: Direct Democracy—Progress and Pitfalls," *IPS News*, (March 16, 2007), http://ipsnews.net/news.asp?idnews=36967.

14 Information from Michael Fox, April 2010.

15 "Creación de los Concejos Vecinales de Montevideo," *Vecinet*, (2006), http://www.chasque.apc.org/vecinet/dconvec.htm.

16 Center for Research on Direct Democracy, "Decentralization and Participatory Democracy in Montevideo, Uruguay: The Role of the Concejos Vecinales," http://www.c2d.ch/inner.php?lname=Research&table=Project&action=current&parent_id=39&link_id=1&sublinkname=current_projects.

17 Clifford Krauss, "The Welfare State Is Alive, if Besieged, in Uruguay," *The New York Times*, (May 3, 1998), http://www.nytimes.com/1998/05/03/world/the-welfare-state-is-alive-if-besieged-in-uruguayhtml.

18 "Banking Crisis Grips Uruguay," *BBC News*, (July 31, 2002), http://news.bbc.co.uk/2/hi/business/2162956.stm.

19 Author interview, March 2005

20 Public Citizen, "Uruguay Bans Water Privatization," 2004, http://www.citizen.org/cmep/Water/cmep_Water/reports/uruguay/.

21 Daniel Renfrew, "Frente Amplio wins elections in Uruguay," *World Socialist Website*, (November 4, 2004), http://www.wsws.org/articles/2004/nov2004/

urug-n04.shtml.

22   Mark Engler, *How to Rule the World: The Coming Battle Over the Global Economy*, (New York: Nation Books, 2008), 267.

23   Quoted in Daniel Chavez, *The New Latin American Left: Utopia Reborn*, (Pluto Press, 2008), 111–112.

24   Bretton Woods Project, "Uruguay announces early IMF repayment," (November 23, 2006), http://www.brettonwoodsproject.org/art-545906.

25   Engler, *How to Rule the World*, 267.

26   Verónica Psetizki, "Laptop for every pupil in Uruguay," *BBC News*, (October 16, 2009), http://news.bbc.co.uk/2/hi/8309583.stm.

27   Marie Trigona, "What Does Bush Want With Uruguay?" *ZNet*, (March 26, 2007), http://www.zmag.org/zspace/commentaries/2882.

28   Dario Montero, "Elections—Uruguay: Landslide Victory for Former Guerilla," *IPS News*, (November 30, 2009), http://ipsnews.net/news.asp?idnews=49469.

29   Angus Reid Global Monitor, "Vázquez Soars as Term Wanes in Uruguay," (October 2, 2009), http://www.angus-reid.com/polls/view/34228/vzquez_soars _as_term_wanes_in_uruguay.

30   Reuters, Afp y Dpa, "Toma posesión el gabinete del presidente José Mujica, en su primer día de gestión," *La Jornada*, (March 3, 2010), http://www.jornada.unam.mx/ 2010/03/03/index.php?section=mundo&article=022n2mun.

31   Quoted in Mercedes López San Miguel, "Vamos a barrer con la indigencia," *Página/12*, (March 2, 2010), http://www.pagina12.com.ar/diario/ elmundo/4-141257-2010-03-02.html.

32   Quoted in Antonio Peredo Leigue, "El Uruguay de Pepe Mujica," *Rebelión*, (October 21, 2009), http://www.rebelion.org/noticia.php?id=93699.

33   Quoted in Yanina Olivera, "Blunt leftist ex-rebel sworn in as Uruguay president," *AFP*, (March 1, 2010), http://www.google.com/hostednews/afp/article/ ALeqM5i7ve8sdN7cnEIPcGcsJHN4SxvKEA.

34   Quoted in "Uruguay: Mujica calls for political dialogue and commitment to Mercosur," *Mercopress*, (March 2, 2010), http://en.mercopress.com/2010/03/02/ uruguay-mujica-calls-for-political-dialogue-and-commitment-to-mercosur.

35   Quoted in Cariboni, "Uruguay."

36   Quoted in Fox, "Uruguay's Frente Amplio."

Chapter Five

1.   Author interview with Jesús Arteaga, 2005.

2   Author interviews with members of Calle y Media, 2005.

3   Quoted in Chesa Boudin, Gabriel Gonzalez, Wilmer Rumbos, *The Venezuelan Revolution: 100 Questions—100 Answers*, (New York: Basic Books, 2006), 66.

4   Author interview with Edgar Lopez, 2005

5   For the full interview with Juan Contreras, see April Howard and Benjamin Dangl, "From a Jail to a Community Radio Station: Revolution in Venezuela Made Tangible," *Toward Freedom*, (September 27, 2006), http://towardfreedom.com/home/content/view/894/

6   Quoted in Carlos Martinez, Michael Fox, and JoJo Farrell, *Venezuela Speaks!: Voices From the Grassroots*, (Oakland: PM Press, 2010), 41.

7   Nikolas Kozloff, *Hugo Chavez: Oil, Politics, and the Challenge to the U.S.*, (New York: Palgrave Macmillan, 2007), 43–45; and Michael McCaughan, *The Battle of Venezuela*, (New York: Seven Stories Press, 2005), 33.

8   Kozloff, *Hugo Chavez*, 43–45. Quote from McCaughan, *The Battle of Venezuela*, 33.

9   Gregory Wilpert, *Changing Venezuela by Taking Power: The History and Policies of the Chavez Government*, (New York: Verso, 2006), 16–17.

10 Kozloff, *Hugo Chavez*, 45–47; and Marta Harnecker, *Hugo Chavez Frias. Un Hombre, Un Pueblo*, (San Sebastián: Gakoa Tercera Prensa, 2002).

11 Wilpert, *Changing Venezuela by Taking Power*, 16–17.

12 Ibid., 17–18; and Martinez, Fox, and Farrell, *Venezuela Speaks*, 299.

13 Steve Ellner, *Empire and Dissent: The United States and Latin America*, (Durham: Duke University Press, 2008), 211–213.

14 Gregory Wilpert, "The Economics, Culture, and Politics of Oil in Venezuela," *Venezuela Analysis* (August 30, 2003), http://www.venezuelanalysis.com/print.php?artno=1000.

15 Cited in Ibid., information from Article 5 of the "Ley Organica de Hidrocarburos."

16 Cited in Wilpert, "The Economics, Culture, and Politics of Oil in Venezuela."

17 David Buchbinder, "Venezuela's oil strike may be over, but industry faces high hurdles," *The Christian Science Monitor*, (February 19. 2003), http://www.csmonitor.com/2003/0219/p07s01-woam.html; Wilpert, "The Economics, Culture, and Politics of Oil in Venezuela."; and "Venezuelan strike falters," *BBC* (January 28, 2003), http://news.bbc.co.uk/2/hi/business/2701873.stm.

18 Author interview with Peggy Ortiz, 2005.

19 Author interview with William Barillas, 2005.

20 Author interview with Yolanda Zerpa, 2005.

21 Author interview with Jesus Gavidia, 2005

22   Quoted in Fred Rosen, *Real World Latin America: A Contemporary Economics and Social Policy Reader*, (Boston: Dollars and Sense, 2009), 13.

23   George Gabriel, "Gender advance in Venezuela: a two-pronged affair," *Open Democracy*, (March 13, 2009), http://www.opendemocracy.net/article/gender-advance-in-venezuela-a-two-pronged-affair.

24   Author interview with Lizarde Prada, 2005.

25   Edgardo Lander, *The New Latin American Left: Utopia Reborn*, (London: Pluto Press, 2008), 82.

26   Mark Engler, *How to Rule the World: The Coming Battle Over the Global Economy*, (New York: Nation Books, 2008), 277; and Fred Rosen, "Sizing Up Hugo Chávez," *Tompaine.com*, (January 25, 2006), http://www.tompaine.com/articles/2006/01/25/sizing_up_hugo_chvez.php.

27   Quoted in Fred Rosen, "Venezuela's New Popular Movements Grow From Above and From Below," *Americas Program*, (November 22, 2005), http://americas.irc-online.org/am/2952.

28   James Petras, "Latin America: Social Movements in Times of Economic Crises," *Axis of Logic*, (August 13, 2009), http://axisoflogic.com/artman/publish/Article_56635.shtml.

29   Sara Motta-Mera, "Social Democracy from Below in Venezuela" in *Reclaiming Latin America: Experiments in Radical Social Democracy*, (London: Zed Books, 2009), 81.

30   Quoted in Ibid., 82.

31   Ibid., 82.

32   Wilpert, *Changing Venezuela by Taking Power*, 66.

33   Yolanda Valery, "Boliburguesía: nueva clase venezolana," *BBC Mundo*, (December 2, 2009), http://www.bbc.co.uk/mundo/economia/2009/12/091202_1045_venezuela_boliburguesia_wbm.shtml.

34   Boudin, Gonzalez, Rumbos, *The Venezuelan Revolution*, 76.

35   Wilpert, *Changing Venezuela by Taking Power*, 59–60.

36   Quoted in Martinez, Fox, and Farrell, *Venezuela Speaks*, 147.

37   For more information on the new communal council law, passed in November of 2009, see James Suggett, "Venezuela's Reformed Communal Council Law Aims at Increasing Participation," *Venezuela Analysis*, (November 25, 2009), http://venezuelanalysis.com/news/4951.

38   Wilpert, *Changing Venezuela by Taking Power*, 59–60.

39   Josh Lerner, "Communal Councils in Venezuela: Can 200 Families Revolutionize Democracy?" *Z Magazine*, (March 6, 2007), http://venezuelanalysis.com/

analysis/2257.

40   Motta, *Reclaiming Latin America*, 84–86.

41   Quoted in Ibid., 84–86.

42   Quoted in Kendra Fehrer Ponniah, "Reconfiguring Democracy: Venezuela's New Communal Councils Confront Bureaucracy," *Peacework Magazine*, (December 2007– January 2008), http://www.peaceworkmagazine.org/print/867.

43   Motta-Mera, *Reclaiming Latin America*, 87–88.

44   Quoted in Martinez, Fox and Farrell, *Venezuela Speaks*, 8.

45   Jonah Gindin, "Chavistas in the Halls of Power, Chavistas in the Streets," in *Dispatches from Latin America: On the Frontlines Against Neoliberalism*, 89.

46   Mary Beth Sheridan, "Chávez Defeats Recall Attempt," *Washington Post*, (August 17, 2004), http://www.washingtonpost.com/wp-dyn/articles/A4208-2004Aug16.html.

47   "Chávez wins Venezuela re-election," *BBC News*, (December 4, 2006), http://news.bbc.co.uk/2/hi/americas/6205128.stm.

48   "Venezuela: 'We are going to resist,'" *Green Left Weekly*, (March 27, 2010), http://www.greenleft.org.au/node/43525; Kiraz Janicke, "Venezuela: Challenges facing the PSUV," *Green Left Weekly*, (October 5, 2007), http://www.greenleft.org.au/node/38418.

49   "Chávez defeated over reform vote," *BBC News*, (December 3, 2007), http://news.bbc.co.uk/2/hi/7124313.stm.

50   Chesa Boudin, "A Silver Lining for the Bolivarian Revolution," *The Nation*, (December 6, 2007), http://www.thenation.com/article/silver-lining-bolivarian-revolution.

51   Boudin, "A Silver Lining for the Bolivarian Revolution."

52   Sujatha Fernandes, "What Does the 'No' Vote Mean?" *The Nation*, (December 6, 2007), http://www.thenation.com/article/what-does-no-vote-mean.

53   For more information on the 2002 coup in Venezuela, see Eva Gollinger, *The Chávez Code: Cracking U.S. Intervention in Venezuela*, (Caracas: Editorial Jose Martí, 2005); and Kim Bartley & Donnacha Ò Briain, *The Revolution Will Not Be Televised*, "Chávez: Inside the Coup" (Del Rey: Vitagraph Films, 2003); Gregory Wilpert, "An Account of April 11–13, 2002, in Venezuela," *Z Communications*, (April 15, 2007), http://www.zcommunications.org/an-account-of-april-11-13-2002-in-venezuela-by-gregory-wilpert; and Ed Vulliamy, "Venezuela coup linked to Bush team," *The Observer*, (April 21, 2002), http://www.guardian.co.uk/world/2002/apr/21/usa.venezuela.

54   Kiraz Janicke, "Venezuela's Co-Managed Inveval: Surviving in a Sea of Capitalism,"

Venezuela Analysis, (July 27, 2007), http://venezuelanalysis.com/analysis/2520.

55 Marie Trigona, "Workers in Control: Venezuela's Occupied Factories," *Venezuela Analysis*, (November 9, 2006), http://venezuelanalysis.com/analysis/2055.

56 Quoted in Ibid.

57 Quoted in Ibid.

58 For further information on Inveval see, Corriente Marxista Revolucionaria, "Venezuela: Inveval workers protest against bureaucratic sabotage," *In Defense of Marxism*, (December 4, 2008), http://www.marxist.com/inveval-workers-protest-against-bureaucratic-sabotage.htm; and Jordi Martorell, "Pointing the way forward," *Morning Star*, (May 21, 2010), http://www.morningstaronline.co.uk/index.php/news/content/view/full/90616.

59 Janicke, "Venezuela's Co-Managed Inveval."

60 Ellner, *Empire and Dissent*, 218-219; and see Jorge Martin, "Venezuela Announces War Against 'Latifundios,'" *Venezuela Analysis*, (January 14, 2005), http://venezuelanalysis.com/analysis/874.

61 Martinez, Fox, and Farrell, *Venezuela Speaks*, 6.

62 Christian Guerrero, "What's So Revolutionary About Venezuelan Coal?" *Earth First! Journal*, (July/August 2005), http://www.earthfirstjournal.org/article.php?id=239.

63 Humberto Márquez, "Venezuelan Indigenous Peoples Protest Coal Mining," *IPS News*, (April 5, 2005), http://www.commondreams.org/headlines05/0405 01.htm.

64 Ibid.

65 Quoted in Paula Palmer, "Coal and Wayuu in Venezuela," *Cultural Survival*, (Winter 2006), http://www.culturalsurvival.org/ourpublications/csq/article/coal-and-wayuu-venezuela.

66 Quoted in Robin Nieto, "The Environmental Cost of Coal Mining in Venezuela," *Venezuela Analysis*, (December 13, 2004), http://venezuelanalysis.com/analysis/835.

67 James Suggett, "Will the Bolivarian Revolution End Coal Mining in Venezuela?," *Venezuela Analysis*, (May 29, 2008), http://venezuelanalysis.com/analysis/3503.

Chapter Six

1 There are a wide variety of social movements and radical church and community groups across the vast country, many of which often collaborate and coordinate with the MST. Due to time, space and the relevance the MST's relation to the government has to the central debate in the book, I focus on the MST here.

2   Land distribution statistic is according to the MST.

3   Quoted in Sue Branford and Jan Rocha, *Cutting the Wire: The Story of the Landless Movement in Brazil*, (London: Latin America Bureau, 2002), 35–36. Encruzilhada Natalino, located near the Fazena Annoni, was the first MST encampment: "History of the MST," *MSTBrazil.org*, http://www.mstbrazil.org/?q=history.

4   Quoted in Branford and Rocha, *Cutting the Wire*, 35–36.

5   Quoted in Ibid., 37–39.

6   As of January 2009, there were 100,000 encampments waiting for land: Michael Fox, "Brazil's Landless Movement Turns 25, Opens 'New Phase' of Struggle," *Upside Down World*, (January 28, 2009), http://upsidedownworld.org/main/content/view/1688/63/.

7   For example at Fazenda Annoni, some families are organized into coops, while others are not and farm their own 20 hectares.

8   Quoted in Branford and Rocha, *Cutting the Wire*, 21–23.

9   "About the MST," MSTBrazil.org, http://www.mstbrazil.org/?q=about.

10   "History of the MST."

11   Richard Plevin, "The World Bank Project Subverts Land Reform in Brazil," *Global Exchange*, (August 6, 1999), http://www.mstbrazil.org/wbsubverts.html.

12   Matthew Flynn, "Brazil's Landless Workers Movement," *Americas Program*, (April 2003), http://americas.irc-online.org/citizen-action/series/06-mst_body.html.

13   Sílvia Leindecker and Michael Fox, *Beyond Elections: Redefining Democracy in the Americas*, (Oakland: PM Press/Estreito Meios Productions, 2008), http://www.beyondelections.com/. Interview from documentary segment at: http://www.youtube.com/watch?v=dK0IAM-DIaA.

14   Quoted in Ibid.

15   Flynn, "Brazil's Landless Workers Movement."

16   Joao Pedro Stédile, "Landless Battalions," *New Left Review*, (May/June 2002), http://www.newleftreview.org/A2390.

17   Ibid.

18   Melissa Moore, "Now It Is Time: The MST and Grassroots Land Reform in Brazil," *Food First*, (March 8, 2003), http://www.foodfirst.org/en/node/49.

19   Quoted in Bill Hinchberger, "The Brazilian Landless Workers Movement (MST)," *The Nation*, (March 2, 1998), http://www.brazilmax.com/news.cfm/tborigem/fe_society/id/29.

20   Angus Lindsay Wright and Wendy Wolford, *To Inherit the Earth: The Landless Movement and the Struggle for a New Brazil*, (Oakland: Food First Books, 2003), 46–51.

21   Quoted in Ibid., 54, 264.

22   Ibid.

23   Branford and Rocha, *Cutting the Wire*, 114–118. At the time of this writing, the MST itinerant schools are being attacked by the local government in Rio Grande do Sul. Government officials claim they are shutting the schools down because they are not officially recognized. For more, see Michael Fox, "Landless Women Launch Protests Across Brazil," *NACLA Report on the Americas*, (March 12, 2009), https://nacla.org/node/5611.

24   Quoted in Branford and Rocha, *Cutting the Wire*, 119. The teacher's name was not provided.

25   Quoted in Marc Saint-Upéry, *El Sueño de Bolívar: El Desafío de Las Izquierdas Sudamericanas*, (Barcelona: Paidós, 2008), 65–67.

26   Stédile, "Landless Battalions."

27   Sue Branford and Bernardo Kucinski, *Lula and the Workers Party in Brazil*, (New York: New Press, 2005), 2.

28   Mark Engler, *How to Rule the World: The Coming Battle Over the Global Economy*, (New York: Nation Books, 2008), 263; and Mario Osava, "Brazil's New President: The Start of a New Dream," *Inter Press Service*, (October 29, 2002), http://www.commondreams.org/headlines02/1029-09.htm.

29   Emir Sader, "Brazil Takes Lula's Measure," in *Dispatches from Latin America: On the Frontlines Against Neoliberalism*, (Boston: South End Press, 2006), 116–118.

30   Mario Osava, "Brazil: The Long Shadow of the Dictatorship," *IPS News*, (September 30, 2009), http://ipsnews.net/news.asp?idnews=48666.

31   Mark Engler, *How to Rule the World*, 263; Osava, "Brazil's New President."

32   Quoted in Branford and Kucinski, *Lula and the Workers Party in Brazil*, 72.

33   Quoted in Ibid., 71.

34   Quoted in Ibid., 28, 36.

35   Ibid., 28, 36.

36   Matthew Flynn, "Alliances Key in the Scramble to Win Brazil's Presidency," *Americas Program*, (June 14, 2002), http://www.cipamericas.org/archives/1268.

37   This point is elaborated on in Michael Fox, "Uruguay's Frente Amplio: From Revolution to Dilution," *Upside Down World*, (June 26, 2007), http://upsidedownworld.org/main/uruguay-archives-48/788-uruguays-frente-amplio-from-revolution-to-dilution.

38   Jeffrey W. Rubin, *Empire and Dissent: The United States and Latin America*, (Durham: Duke University Press, 2008), 177.

39   Sader, *Dispatches from Latin America*, 122–123.

40   Quoted in Sue Branford, "The Lula Government in Brazil: The End of a Dream," in *Reclaiming Latin America*, 152.

41   Sader, *Dispatches from Latin America*, 122–123.

42   Branford, *Reclaiming Latin America*, 157.

43   Sader, *Dispatches from Latin America*, 124.

44   Francisco de Oliveira, "Lula in the Labyrinth," *New Left Review*, (November–December, 2006), http://www.newleftreview.org/?view=2642.

45   Leslie Evans, "One Year of the Lula Administration,". UCLA International Institute, (April 28, 2004), http://www.international.ucla.edu/article.asp?parentid=10711.

46   Quoted in interview with João Pedro Stédile, in *Revista PUC-VIVA*, 19, (São Paulo: Feb-April 2003), cited in Branford and Kucinski, *Lula and the Workers Party in Brazil*, 106.

47   Quoted in Chris Tilly, Marie Kennedy and Tarso Luís Ramos, "Land Reform Under Lula: One Step Forward, One Step Back," *Dollars and Sense*, (2009), http://www.dollarsandsense.org/archives/2009/1009kennedyramostilly.html.

48   Rubin, *Empire and Dissent* 163, 171.

49   Quoted in Gibby Zobel,"We are millions," *The New Internationalist*, (December 1, 2009), http://www.newint.org/features/special/2009/12/01/we-are-millions/.

50   Harry Vanden, *Real World Latin America: A Contemporary Economics and Social Policy Reader*, (Boston: Dollars and Sense, 2009), 173.

51   Félix Sánchez, João Machado Borges Neto, and Rosa Maria Marques, *The New Latin American Left: Utopia Reborn*, (London: Pluto Press, 2008), 54.

52   Quoted in Tilly, Kennedy and Ramos. "Land Reform Under Lula."

53   Fox, "Brazil's Landless Movement Turns 25."

54   Quoted in Christine Crowley, "Lula No Long Ball Hitter When it Comes to Land Reform," *Council on Hemispheric Affairs*, (April 7, 2006), http://www.coha.org/lula-no-long-ball-hitter-when-it-comes-to-land-reform/.

55   Sánchez, Neto, and Marques, *The New Latin American Left*, 54–55.

56   Quoted in Ibid., 64–65.

57   Crowley, "Lula No Long Ball Hitter When it Comes to Land Reform."

58   Fox, "Brazil's Landless Movement Turns 25."

Chapter Seven

1   Quoted in "Ex ministro fue la mano derecha de Stroessner, dice obispo," *ABC Color*, (May 2, 2009), http://archivo.abc.com.py/2009-05-02/articulos/517905/

ex-ministro-fue-la-mano-derecha-de-stroessner-dice-obispo.

2 Quoted in "Volvió Montanaro y con él la represión," *Jaku'éke Paraguay*, http://www.jakueke.com/articulo.php?ID=8930.

3 "Represor regresa a Paraguay por enfermedad," *TeleSur*, http://www.telesurtv.net/noticias/secciones/nota/48894-NN/represor-regresa-a-paraguay-por-enfermedad/.

4 Raúl Zibechi, "Paraguay's Hour of Change," *Americas Program*, (September 24, 2007), http://americas.irc-online.org/am/4572/.

5 Author interview with Tomas Palau in March 2007. Also see April Howard and Benjamin Dangl, "Dissecting the Politics of Paraguay's Next President," *Toward Freedom*, (April 10, 2008), http://towardfreedom.com/home/content/view/1280/1/.

6 Howard and Dangl, "Dissecting the Politics of Paraguay's Next President."

7 Diego González, "Lugo's Dilemmas," *Americas Program*, (September 26, 2009), http://americas.irc-online.org/am/6455.

8 Discussion with Galeano, *La Soja Mata*, http://www.lasojamata.org/en/node/235.

9 Author interview Leticia Galeano in April 2009.

10 Quoted in "Miles de campesinos marchan en Asunción para reclamar a Lugo un mayor compromiso en la reforma agrarian," *Europa Press*, (March 25, 2010), http://www.europapress.es/latam/paraguay/noticia-paraguay-miles-campesinos-marchan-asuncion-reclamar-lugo-mayor-compromiso-reforma-agraria-20100325170417.html.

11 Quoted in "Campesinos paraguayos marchan por eterno reclamo reforma agrarian," *Reuters*, (March 25, 2010), http://lta.reuters.com/article/domesticNews/idLTASIE62O0LJ20100325?pageNumber=2&virtualBrandChannel=0.

12 "Exclusive: Paraguayan President Fernando Lugo on US Relations in Latin America, the Iraq War, Liberation Theology and Being the 'Bishop of the Poor,'" *Democracy Now!*, (September 23, 2008), http://www.democracynow.org/2008/9/23/exclusive_paraguayan_president_fernando_lugo_on.

13 Author interview with Orlando Castillo in May 2009.

14 Quoted in Natalia Ruiz Díaz, "Paraguay: Rural Associations Protest Land Occupations," *IPS News*, (December 15, 2008), http://ipsnews.net/news.asp?idnews=45124.

15 Quintín Nicolás Riquelme Cantero, *Los Sin Tierra en Paraguay: Conflictos Agrarios y Movimiento Campesino*, (Buenos Aires: Consejo Latinoamericano de Ciencias Sociales, 2003), 49–52.

16 Quoted in Ibid., 54–55.

17   Ibid., 60.

18   Discussion with Galeano, *La Soja Mata*, http://www.lasojamata.org/en/node/235.

19   Javiera Rulli, *United Soya Republics: The Truth About Soya Production in South America*, (Buenos Aires: Grupo Reflexión Rural), 221–234. The book is available online at http://lasojamata.iskra.net/en/node/91.

20   González, "Lugo's Dilemmas." See also Pablo Stefanoni "Época en Paraguay," *Le Monde Diplomatique* South American edition (July 2007).

21   Andrew Nickson, "Paraguay: Fernando Lugo vs the Colorado machine," *Open Democracy*, (February 28, 2008), http://www.opendemocracy.net/article/democracy_power/politics_protest/paraguay_fernando_lugo.

22   Marco Castillo, Regina Kretschmer, Javiera Rulli, and Gaby Schwartzmann, "Paraguay: Campesino Leader Charged For Confronting Crop Spraying," *La Soja Mata*, (March 27, 2008), http://upsidedownworld.org/main/content/view/1198/1/.

23   Misión internacional de observación al Paraguay, *Informe 2006*, p. 6; SERPAJ Paraguay.

24   April Howard and Benjamin Dangl, "The Multinational Beanfield War: Soy cultivation spells doom for Paraguayan campesinos," *In These Times*, (April 12, 2007), http://www.inthesetimes.com/article/3093/the_multinational_beanfield_war/.

25   Nickson, "Paraguay: Fernando Lugo vs the Colorado machine."

26   Quoted in Castillo, Kretschmer, Rulli and Schwartzmann, "Paraguay: Campesino Leader Charged For Confronting Crop Spraying."

27   Howard and Dangl, "Dissecting the Politics of Paraguay's Next President."

28   Author interview with Gilda Roa in April 2009.

29   Javiera Rulli, "Massacre in Paraguay," *Upside Down World*, (July 17, 2005), http://upsidedownworld.org/main/content/view/45/44/.

30   Rulli, *United Soya Republics*, 221–234.

31   Quoted in BASE-IS, "The Battle of Tekojoja, Paraguay," *La Soja Mata*, http://www.lasojamata.org/node/15.

32   Author interview with Virginia Barrientos in April 2009.

33   Author interview with Isabel Rivas in April 2009.

34   Quoted in Raúl Zibechi, "Asunción's Bañados Neighborhood: The Power of Community," *Americas Program*, (August 7, 2008), http://americas.irc-online.org/am/5451.

35   Author interview with Carmen Castillo in April 2009. And see Zibechi, "Asunción's Bañados Neighborhood."

36   Author interview with Patricio in April 2009.

37   Author interview with "Don" in April 2009.

Chapter Eight

1   "Chomsky on Obama," *Examiner.com*, (November 21, 2008), http://www.examiner
.com/x-928-DC-Politics-Examiner~y2008m11d21-Chomsky-on-Obama.

2   Howard Zinn, "Election Madness," *The Progressive*, (March 2008), http://www.
progressive.org/mag_zinn0308.

3   Howard Zinn, *A People's History of the United States*, (New York: Harper Peren-
nial, 2001), 392.

4   Emma Goldman, "Anarchism: What It Really Stands For," *Anarchy Archives*,
http://dwardmac.pitzer.edu/ANARCHIST_ARCHIVES/goldman/aando/
anarchism.html.

5   Ziga Vodovnik, "Howard Zinn: Anarchism Shouldn't Be a Dirty Word," *Coun-
terPunch*, (May 17, 2008), http://www.alternet.org/news/85427/.

6   Turbulence Collective, *What Would It Mean To Win?*, (Oakland: PM Press, 2010),
100, 104.

7   Kari Lydersen, *Revolt On Goose Island. The Chicago Factory Takeover, and What it
Says About the Economic Crisis*, (Brooklyn: Melville House, 2009), 67–72.

8   Ibid., 89–90.

9   Ibid., 57–58, 62–65.

10 Ibid., 87.

11 Liz Miller, *The Water Front*, documentary, (Bullfrog Films, 2007), http://
www.waterfrontmovie.com/.

12 Ibid.

13 Ibid.

14 Jesu Estrada, "The Struggle For Water In Detroit: An Interview With Marian Kramer," *People's Tribune*, (March 6, 2009), http://www.peoplestribune.org/
PT.2009.03/PT.2009.03.06.html.

15 Yvett Moore, "A Cold Shoulder for Detroit's Working Poor," *Response*, http://
gbgm-umc.org/Response/articles/detroit.html#Yvette.

16 Estrada, "The Struggle For Water In Detroit."

17 Miller, "The Water Front."

18 Maureen D. Taylor, "A victory in the struggle for affordable water," *People's Tribune*, (March, 2007), http://www.peoplestribune.org/PT.2007.03/
PT.2007.03.3.html

19 Miller, "The Water Front."

20   "Fiascos: Atlanta, Georgia," *Public Citizen*, http://www.citizen.org/cmep/Water/us/municipal/atlanta/articles.cfm?ID=9211.

21   Douglas Jehl, "As Cities Move to Privatize Water, Atlanta Steps Back," *New York Times*, (February 10, 2003), http://www.nytimes.com/2003/02/10/us/as-cities-move-to-privatize-water-atlanta-steps-back.html?pagewanted=all.

22   "Fiascos: Atlanta, Georgia," *Public Citizen.*

23   Jon R. Luoma, "Water for Profit," *Mother Jones*, (November/December 2002), http://motherjones.com/politics/2002/11/water-profit.

24   Ibid.

25   Paul Reyes,"Opportunity Knocks," *The Virginia Quarterly Review*, (Fall 2009), http://www.vqronline.org/articles/2009/fall/reyes-opportunity-knocks/.

26   Max Rameau, *Take Back The Land: Land, Gentrification and the Umoja Village Shantytown*, (CreateSpace, 2008), 59–62.

27   Information from the Take Back the Land website, http://takebacktheland.org/.

28   Rameau, *Take Back The Land*, 7.

29   Reyes,"Opportunity Knocks."

30   Information from the Take Back the Land website, http://takebacktheland.org/.

31   Rick Jervis, "Homeless turn foreclosures into shelters," *USA Today*, http://www.usatoday.com/news/nation/2008-12-10-homesquatters_N.htm.

32   John Leland, "With Advocates' Help, Squatters Call Foreclosures Home," *New York Times*, (April 9, 2009), http://www.nytimes.com/2009/04/10/us/10squatter.html.

33   Tristram Korten, "Foreclosure Nation: Squatters or Pioneers?," *Mother Jones*, (May/June 2008), http://motherjones.com/politics/2008/05/foreclosure-nation-squatters-or-pioneers.

34   "Activist moves homeless into foreclosures," *Associated Press*, (December 1, 2008), http://www.msnbc.msn.com/id/28002276/.

35   Ibid.

36   Max Rameau, "Take Back the Land," *Left Turn*, (May 1, 2009), http://www.leftturn.org/?q=node/1308.

Index

Photo by Joshua Lambert

Benjamin Dangl has worked as a journalist covering politics and social issues across Latin America for nearly a decade, writing for *The Guardian Unlimited*, *The Nation*, *The Progressive*, *Utne Reader*, *In These Times*, *Alternet*, *Z Magazine*, and dozens of other media outlets. Dangl has received two Project Censored Awards for his investigative reports on US government and military intervention in Latin America, and has been interviewed by a variety of news networks such as the BBC and programs including *Democracy Now!*

He teaches Latin American history and globalization at Burlington College in Vermont, and is the editor of TowardFreedom.com, a progressive perspective on world events. He is the founder and editor of UpsideDownWorld.org, a publication on politics and social movements in Latin America, and the author of the book *The Price of Fire: Resource Wars and Social Movements in Bolivia* (AK Press, 2007).

For more information and collected writing, visit www.BenDangl.net/.

Support AK Press!

AK Press is one of the world's largest and most productive anarchist publishing houses. We're entirely worker-run and democratically managed. We operate without a corporate structure—no boss, no managers, no bullshit. We publish close to twenty books every year, and distribute thousands of other titles published by other like-minded independent presses from around the globe.

The Friends of AK program is a way that you can directly contribute to the continued existence of AK Press, and ensure that we're able to keep publishing great books just like this one! Friends pay a minimum of $25 per month, for a minimum three month period, into our publishing account. In return, Friends automatically receive (for the duration of their membership), as they appear, one free copy of every new AK Press title. They're also entitled to a 20% discount on everything featured in the AK Press Distribution catalog and on the website, on any and every order. You or your organization can even sponsor an entire book if you should so choose!

There's great stuff in the works—so sign up now to become a Friend of AK Press, and let the presses roll!

Won't you be our friend? Email friendsofak@akpress.org for more info, or visit the Friends of AK Press website: http://www.akpress.org/programs/friendsofak